A WORLD BOLD AS LOVE

ROCK

A WORLD BOLD AS LOVE

ROCK

PHOTOGRAPHED AND EDITED BY

Douglas Kent Hall

FROM INTERVIEWS BY

Sue C. Clark

COWLES BOOK COMPANY, INC.

NEW YORK

To
Claire
and
Ralph J. Gleason,
a friend

SBN 402-12591-6
Library of Congress Catalog Card Number 70-108993
Cowles Book Company, Inc.
A subsidiary of Cowles Communications, Inc.
Published simultaneously in Canada by
    General Publishing Company, Ltd.
    30 Lesmill Road, Don Mills, Toronto, Ontario
Printed in the United States of America
First Edition

PREFACE

This book is designed to reflect the vitality, the integrity, and the simple purity of the rock world—that is, to take this world on its own terms. The photographs and interview statements are presented like raw materials for an epic poem or collage about one of the most spectacularly significant and profoundly puzzling cultural manifestations in the history of this country. It is tempting to tamper with them, to take them and refine them until they have the feel of a book about a more ordinary and a less elusive subject. But to warp these materials into a form in which they say what I might like them to say or hope they are saying would be to subscribe to the folly of many—if not most—critics of rock music and culture and would be to commit a serious injustice to the performers and their audiences. Besides, with a subject as new and transitory as rock it is too easy to make mere pretentiousness look like truth.

Literally hundreds of persons participated in the making of this book. Many of them are represented in the following pages. And for their efforts and the efforts of their press representatives Sue and I would like to give our sincere thanks. Some performers are not included simply because circumstances were against it. A number of other performers can thank their management for saving them the trouble of being here.

Most of the photographs were taken during October, November, and December of 1969, in New York City, Boston, San Francisco, Los Angeles, Portland, Seattle, and Paris, France. The interviews were done between September and December, 1969, in New York and San Francisco. Special thanks go to Bill Graham and Kip Cohen of the Fillmores West and East. Light show patterns in any of the photographs are the work of the incomparable Joshua Light Show.

Doing this book has thoroughly reaffirmed my belief in the future of this country. For a long time, America has been selling out; and now, finally, a new kind of culture is emerging that refuses to accept those false ideals we have so patently been assured represent the ultimate in freedom and integrity. In short, young Americans cannot be convinced that this is the best of all possible worlds. Rock culture and its minstrel heroes are seeking something better. Evidence of this quest can be seen in the songs, in the audience response. Songs are no longer being crafted of empty lyrics that simply fit a compelling rhythmical pattern; and the audience is no longer willing to overlook glossy, inane rhymes for the heavy mesmerizing beat that used to carry most of pop music. Important questions are being asked; solutions are being sought. And in this manifestation of serious concern I see something promising, something hopeful: that Rock *is* a world bold as love.

DOUGLAS KENT HALL

A WORLD BOLD AS LOVE

ROCK

The Music

Music is everybody's mother. Music is your whole life. Music is like your blood. Music is a part of you. Everything you do is in rhythms. When you look at a beautiful piece of film without music: nothin'. Put music with any shot and suddenly you lift up and you're in some poetic thing.

Donovan

Rock and roll is beautiful and it's ugly simultaneously. I mean, it's rock and roll that brings people together in the mud in Woodstock. It's rock and roll that starts black riots in Rochester and has cops beating people on the head for ten hours later. It's rock and roll, you know; there's so many good things, and so many bad things. It's so unpredictable. It's so exciting and spontaneous. I think culturally it's not the way you study Beethoven and find a cultural position for it. It's just that it is the culture. It grows. And chances are that you watch rock and roll moving and going. And chances are that it's the culture that's with it. So you can't find a place for it in culture. It just exists. It's spontaneous and it changes—changes daily.

Howard Stein

I feel an affinity with the tradition of poetry itself. Today we call it pop and Paul McCartney is a pop musician, but really he's of the folk tradition inasmuch as it's centuries, thousands of years old. Once upon a time, there were universities that you went to and you learned poetry as an art and it was religious. And it's strange that I just write songs and I'm here and I'm the center of so much attraction. And records sell millions and millions of records. And all the fame and fortune—what is it? What's it all about? Well, it's a very beautiful thing because it's music. Music, records, pop, dollars, but it's music—it's the sound of the universe. It's the sound of everything: love, peace. With music they start wars. With music they stir people into frenzy. With music they make people peaceful. With music they sell products. It's great. It's much more important than the superficial plastic of album covers, it's a whole business. Why? Because it's a tradition that's always been kept up. And the poet can make vibrations in the atmosphere that millions can pick up who can't say that vibration and return it, and maybe in Madison Square Garden—if any of you here come, you'll get an inclination of what you can do with many people thinking one thing. And your poets and your painters and your artists can release those things. And it's a needed thing. You need lots of poets to release tensions and create things.

Donovan

Every artist I know is on a positive trip, man. They're not depicting doom and destruction, they're out there saying let's start something new! I want to start something new and I'm ready to work for it. Here, let me turn my hand to it, man. And they're not afraid to really turn their hand to it. It's really true. People are startin' to really get off. Learnin' to get off, learnin' to have a good time. That's hard enough. I mean those people are really havin' a lot of trouble learning how to really have a good time. Not do plastic trips that are imposed from a superficial preconception from a magazine or something, but find out what really pleases you and do it. That's the part that's best communicated by the music. And it works, man. 'Cause when we play, man, people feel like that.

David Crosby/Crosby, Stills, Nash and Young

Donovan

I think now music is setting the standard for the way people live, because it goes into so many homes. It's over all the media. When it excites Madison Avenue and is played behind commercials for soft drinks and food and what have you, I think it plays an important part. I remember back in the fifties, when comedians doing variety shows on TV would make fun or tease and they would get big laughter out of imitating the groups. They couldn't understand what the kids were singing, the doo-wahs or the ba-dum-ba-dum-ba-dum-ba-dum-ba (sings) yip-yip-yip-yip. But music has changed. The kids are very serious. Their songs carry a message that could be political; it could be about life; it could be about religion; it could be about an event in the paper; it could be about the war in Vietnam; it could be about integration—black or white, yellow or red. I think it's very serious-minded.

Kelly Isley/The Isley Brothers

A lot more people are into playing, and a lot more people encouraged to get into music. It's provided employment for a lot of people who otherwise are chronic unemployables mostly. It's the look of it, and a few of the catch phrases of the San Francisco thing has developed where you can find it all over the country and you can hear it anywhere there's kids, and probably just about everywhere.

Jerry Garcia/The Grateful Dead

I don't think you can divide humanity into the young and the old. The more important distinction is like the old story of the ant and the grasshopper. In every human being there is a conflict like the ant and the grasshopper . . . to play and work . . . and more or less, we are all afflicted with this conflict. Music appeals to the grasshoppers. They might be as hardworking as anyone. Just the way many older people tend toward the working style, there are some that tend toward the playing style. Music appeals to the grasshoppers—it's a change from the daily grind. It provides an alternative. It's not so dim as the ant style.

Jim Morrison/The Doors

Felix Pappalardi

I see basically that music is becoming more "earthy." I think we've gotten out of the fantasy stage of music. We're not singin' about the moon and the stars an' the sleepy lagoons and that sort of stuff. "Moon River" was a different kind of thing. "Moon River" I think was successful because of the melody and the fact that it was associated with the motion picture. That kind of told the whole story that "Moon River" just hinted at. I think that was a different time, a different period, a different kind of scene. But now people are talking about "Everyday People" and "Who's Makin' Love to Your Old Lady," I mean, which is really where it's at, because these are the problems that you run into every day.

I think music going back to the time of the story-teller, you know, when the music was music because it said something to all of the people. It's basically becoming what country and western and rhythm and blues always has been. The music of the people. They've given it a lot of funny names—they've called it "folk music" and then they called it somethin' else, and now they want to call it "psychedelic." But I think what it all boils down to is this: it's still gonna be rhythm and blues and country and western. Music that the average Joe can understand and relate to.

Jerry Butler

I'm against puttin' all names on music. It just causes more confusion. Like you can say "voodoo rock" . . . but it's all music. What I play is music. What everybody plays is music. If it's symphonic or it's jazz, it's still music. It don't make no difference if it's hillbilly or rock and roll or what, because it's still music. If you like it, it's good. If you don't like it, it's bad. It's bad to you. That's your own personal taste. I like music to just be natural however it comes out. Like, it might not be the greatest, but if it's natural, it's a good feel, it's better to me than anything that's all fancy and got all kind of froufrous in it that don't really mean nothin'.

Dr. John, the Night Tripper

David Crosby

When you go out on a stage, the first thing that hits me is that all these people came here to do something that they hardly ever do in the whole course of their living day—is to open the minds totally to something. Very few people do that. They'll open their mind to a degree and remain hesitant about one area. But when they come and listen to a band, especially if they're sitting down, they're just wide open. That's a really heavy respect that they pay to come and open up their mind to you. And most people are kind of scared to do that at any other kind of way, except to a music, or a play or something, that they have faith that who-ever's there isn't going to hurt them, you know. They're going to put something down, so they open it up. But like they wouldn't do it to a cab driver or a bus, you know, a counterman. When you go out there and you realize that all those people came to give you that, to pay you that respect, that they're going to sit there and let you do it to them, man, you know, that's usually what's on my mind.

Dino Valente/Quicksilver Messenger Service

I'm very surprised at some of the music that's out, because I just can't see people appreciating some of the music that I hear. I can understand that some people have "ignorant ears." When I say "ignorant ears" I don't mean with it being physical, but I mean like havin' an "ignorant ear," like they don't pick the part or they don't listen to the melody or they don't listen to a specific part; they're listening to the boom-boom-boom and they'll come up and they'll say, "Hey! That's a hit."

Sam Moore/Sam & Dave

The music of today changes. Now kids listen to words, they listen to lyrics, and they listen to the arrangement around a song. A long time back, maybe five or ten years ago, they would like just listen to the beat, and if the beat was good, they didn't care what the cut was saying. They'd just buy the record. But they grew up and now they listen.

Sam Gooden/The Impressions

All those kids are from America. And they're all incredible. And on top of that, all them kids want to have a good time, because they're from America. Because America isn't a good time. They're kids— they're bodies—they just want a little action—a little fun. Kids haven't been dancin' for a long time. We're concerned with the kids. Just being kids ourselves not too long ago, they're who we want to reach, who we relate to. We're just convinced that kids are the furthest out, because they're the youngest and they're really fresh, man.

Robin/MC 5

I see music kind of broken up into small sections. The business side of a rock band, and a rock band as musicians, and a rock band as entertainers are all different facets of the same game and they all have their own points. I don't think music alone will get anybody anywhere. So there is a lot of showmanship developing and some of it is getting very forced. I find the people that are saying serious things musically, unless they've got a particular angle, don't get the exposure that they deserve.

Alvin Lee/Ten Years After

John Sebastian

Robin Tyner

Everybody's got a different musical note. Everybody gives off a certain musical note. What am I? I think I'm F-sharp. The thing is if you can go around and you meet somebody who's in F-sharp, you're in harmony, see. But if you meet somebody who's in F—unnng—it's a discord: you don't get on.

The wind is in chords.

Donovan

The kids dig it because it does something to you. Oh, yes, they love to dance. That's the joy that they have. They love to dance and they are really getting it. They are doing their thing all over the world and it's beautiful.

Little Richard

There's good music and there's bad music. I intend to spend a lot of time in the former category. I believe that what's going to happen will be initiated by individual musicians rather than cults.

That's the thing about contemporary music. People have the audacity to lay down to everybody else in the country and the world who is important and who isn't important. And it might be well for these people to know, if they had any education, any musical education, I mean, and I'm a stickler about that, 'cause I don't believe that they do, is that Johann Sebastian Bach was rated eleventh of composers in Europe in 1735. He died in 1750 and emerges today, of course, as the greatest of the era. So I believe that criticism and critics, they've always been the same. They're full of shit. If they weren't, they'd be out playin' and they wouldn't have time to criticize anybody.

Felix Pappalardi/Mountain

Little Richard

Dr. John

Jerry Goodman

I'm a musician. I'm into music. Music is an old trip with me, still is, dig it. Maybe that's the thing; it's something you can go whole hog in, put your whole other total self into.

Jerry Garcia/The Grateful Dead

There are only two universal languges: music and math. And they're very close to each other. And believe me, everybody knows, when we start boogiein', what's going on. I mean, we can play it to Bushmen, and we can play it to Gobi Desert riders, we can play it to people from Paris, man. They all understand that kah-dum-dum-plah, kah-dum-dum-plah, da-du-du-blahm. They all heard it. They can't sit still to it. They don't know how to tell you what it is. They probably don't know the name, but *everybody* can feel music. They can all feel the emotional surge you get, man, when somebody cuts two harmony lines that are just perfectly in tune, and turns 'em like dolphins. Just does something, just heartrending. That's an emotional thing to *anyone!*

David Crosby/Crosby, Stills, Nash and Young

Music is a safe type of high. It's more the way it's supposed to be. That's where highness came, I guess, from anyway. It's nothing but rhythm and motion.

Jimi Hendrix

The most important thing about rock is the why of rock. The most important aspect is where it comes from. What makes a young person make such a statement? Why do they turn to music to make such a statement? And to do that we sort of really have to examine the sociological phenomenon and the impact of the forties and fifties, mainly the fifties, which, of course, were so extraordinarily repressive and where people were honestly scared. I think back to my school days when a teacher said something that was law. It never as much as entered my mind that you could say, "Wait, that doesn't make much sense." There was a whole atmosphere then when certain things were told and the values, the sexual values and whatever, were accepted without question.

And the dichotomy started hitting me. That here is what society and what the system tell me is real. And then there are those feelings, those feelings that I have of being. There is the human relations—there are emotional hang-ups, an emotional search. There are all of these things which somehow that machine doesn't talk about very much. A machine that kills, a machine that lies, a machine that alters for its own means and whatever, the natural dichotomy started hitting me. And where did I hear people echoing these sentiments was certainly not from the system, but, of course, from literature from time immemorial.

Lorin Hollander

Jimi Hendrix

Rock is the only national alternate medium. Rock is the only medium of the alternate culture that exists on a national basis. The alternate culture occupies some time on radio, but that's locally. Underground papers are local. I'd like to see a national underground paper, a true national underground paper . . . but not having that, we have the music, the records. That's the medium, so it's most important.

Danny Fields

I think it also stems from the fact that music is coming more from the mind and the mind is just weird, and there are just so many ultimate possibilities and therefore music should too. It reflects the mind, and I think as people get higher, music will get higher.

Jerry Goodman and Jerry Smith/The Flock

Music shouldn't be picked apart too much unless you're really teaching folklore at UCLA or something.
John Kay/Steppenwolf

Music is a universal language. Any country you go to understands it and it's really powerful because I found out like many years ago when we used to have an organ that was the size of this room, that you can really control people by music. Like you could take them up to here or drop them down to here. You can really control the mob if you have enough electricity. Jimi Hendrix is certainly doing it because he takes them—wherever he wants—he takes them. It's a very, very powerful force. You can call it God, because it's an intangible force that is hard to explain.

Felix Cavaliere/The Rascals

Rock is so much fun. You can do that. You just lay out there and just jam. That's what it's all about —filling up the chest cavities and the empty knee-caps and the elbows!

Jimi Hendrix

The Strata of Rock

Jimi Hendrix

I don't like to be misunderstood by anything or anybody. So if I want to wear a red bandanna and turquoise slacks and if I want hair down to my ankles, well, that's me. They don't know what's running through my blood. Shit, I'm representing everything as far as I'm concerned.

Jimi Hendrix

Jimi Hendrix

Jimi Hendrix is a genius. I think he's the most important musician that perhaps has come out of the rock scene. For a start technically he's ridiculously good. He's able to do so much with the technique. His creative mind is better or as good as his technique. He has so much music inside him, the same way Django Reinhardt could play anything that would come into his head. His technique would not restrict him at all. So when you get that coupling, it's a rare combination, and it's just a weird sort of situation that Jimi being put as a showman or entertainer, and perhaps coming up too fast in the public adoration, has sort of crippled things a bit because they've tended to miss the point of how good a musician he is and can get it confused with the sensational aspect of his performances and the sensational aspects of his image.

I haven't seen him for about a year, but I know that he was always gettin' pretty upset about the fact that people would put pressures on him to play the hits. If he'd do a performance, he would really go onstage on any night—"All of you people, there's hundreds and thousands of you, and you've come to see me, but have you really come to see me or have you just come to see Jimi Hendrix 'star' and you want to hear 'Foxy Lady' and you want to hear this, or do you really want to see me try and give you some music that I want to play?" And nine out of ten, Jimi comes onstage with that feeling that he wants to play for those people because they've presumably come to hear him and his musical mind. And they don't want to know about it. So he would end up, he would play a couple of things that they knew, and he would play a slow blues for himself, and it would be to any musician's ears a completely mind-blowing and really creative thing that would be so complete and good. And the audience would still shout for those other things. So when he hears that, he's really felt that he's poured something out

and that's the real him as a musician, and they haven't even known about it. So he just gets bitter about it—"Okay, you want this, you got it, blam, blam, blam. I'm through and that's it!"

John Mayall

I think Hendrix is underrated for the step he's taken and the changes he's made in contemporary music. He came in with a very new thing, a very new way of saying something. I think he'd score full marks for originality, which isn't too common nowadays. He's not accepted as that original thing. He kinda gets put into a pop-rock bag, probably from his flamboyancy of the early days.

The thing is if you do anything vaguely representing Hendrix it sounds like you're playing like Hendrix. He's got it so down to earth. His style is so original that either you're playing like him or you're not. He is a definite live force on his own.

I don't even think of Hendrix as black. Hendrix is Hendrix.

Alvin Lee/Ten Years After

I dig Hendrix a lot because he really has a lot of control over his instrument. He's really strong. And I like his singing, too.

The people who are digging Hendrix are digging him for different reasons than I dig him. Most people dig him because of his sensational showmanship. I like that, too. I like showmanship. I think it's a good thing. Because if the people don't know that much about music, and they're out there spending that money, I think it's just a beautiful thing that they should want to spend their time and money digging music instead of going to a movie. If that gives them just a little more pleasure than they would have got out of the music by itself, I can dig it. I'm a musician and I can see what Jimi Hendrix is doing musically and I dig that, too.

Elvin Bishop

Jimi Hendrix, I think, was probably the first that combined real talent with real volume, which is probably the beginning. I don't think anyone was really into it. I feel it was very physical—very physical and very mental, very moving. Puts you through changes. And his lyrics, very heavy lyrics.

Jerry Goodman and Jerry Smith/The Flock

He's really a big influence. To me he's the present-day Chuck Berry. Chuck Berry was the Jimi Hendrix of those days. He's come up with more original things than anybody I can think of on the guitar. The whole feedback fuzz thing he does and just the whole concept of the way he plays is so different that it's fantastic. From what I've seen of Jimi, his music seems to pretty well project his personality. I don't know. I hear more people copying Eric Clapton than I do Jimi Hendrix, but Eric Clapton isn't as original as Jimi Hendrix is, to me, because he's more or less basic blues, and Jimi Hendrix just seems to be a little more original to me.

Johnny Winter

I think right now Jimi's the greatest young blues guitarist. A couple of things really fascinate me about Jimi. John Hammond noticed this, too. In fact, Johnny really noticed Jimi before anybody did. Jimi was working down at the Cafe Wha! as Jimi James and the Blue Flames—three or four fairly terrible musicians and Jimi, who was just scary, you know. So Johnny heard him and started using him in his band, having him play guitar. I remember the first time I went to hear Johnny with the Screamin' Night Hawks, and Jimi was playing guitar with him; it just tore my head off. The thing that's peculiar about Jimi is that he has the greatest sense of the blues mode that I know; he understands the modes of the blues better than anybody that I know. It's very, very easy for all of these blues guitar players these days to simply make mistakes as they run through all of their various references. They play a little B. B., they play a little Albert King or something. But in all of these kind of little references that all these cats play, they very, very frequently just make mistakes. They play a wrong note. They play a kind of major-y blues lick in a minorish blues mode. I mean, it's hard to describe. I'm talking about a wrong note, right? Jimi doesn't play those. He just doesn't. But at the same time the people that Jimi admires most are people like Bobby Dylan, and like he really dug John Hammond and wanted to get Johnny Hammond records, and he really learned a lot of old blues off John Hammond records. So in a lot of ways Jimi is really unique second-generation. Because with all this incredible blues instinct, you know, a lot of the people that he really digs are completely in another genre.

I've heard several, several tunes that he's written that really really move me. The thing that I like best is his delivery of tunes, which is also completely unique: he doesn't always sing completely. Sometimes, like the other night I was riding around New York with him and Cass, and Cass was rapping about "Castles Are Made of Sand," and "You son of a bitch, you don't sing that song. You do something else with that song." And Jimi was saying, "Yeah," and he says to me, "You have to kind of pretend, like you have to sing it like you was almost falling asleep." That's the way he spoke of arriving at the way to sing it. It's really true 'cause a lot of it is just a—it's almost—a style of reading poetry rather than a completely singer's approach.

John Sebastian

Jimi Hendrix

There are a lot of people that would like to be like him. That would like to sound like him. There are a lot of people that would like to be him. So that means you got a big influence on music . . . like James Brown. . . . There's people who would like to be like you and be you, really, if that were possible. Then they start living like you, they like what you like, they play what you like, they like what you play, they live like you, they play like you, they dress like you, they wear their hair, they follow you . . . It's obvious.

Sly Stone/Sly and the Family Stone

Jimi Hendrix

Jimi Hendrix

He had that soul, that electrifying filler, that blues touch, that he has now, but didn't nobody know him. Jimi Hendrix is playing old music but a new sound, but what he's really playing is old blues.

Little Richard

Jimi. I dig what he does. Like it seems to me from some of the things I heard Jimi do on his albums, it's not a "I love you, do you love me, too?"—that rhyming type thing. He just tells the story—like what's happening every day. But he's weird with it. You got to be deep to dig it. That's the way I look at it. And I like people to be free.

Gladys Knight and the Pips

Three or four different worlds went by within the wink of an eye. Things were happening. There was this cat came around called Black Gold. And there was this other cat came around called Captain Coconut. Other people came around. I was all these people. And finally when I went back home, all of a sudden I found myself bein' a little West Coast Seattle boy—for a second. Then all of a sudden when you're back on the road again, there he goes, he starts goin' back. That's my life until somethin' else comes about.

There are a lot of things you have to sacrifice. It all depends on how deep you want to get into whatever your gig is. Whatever you're there for. So like the deeper you get into it the more sacrifices you have to do, maybe even on your personality or your outward this and that. I just dedicate my whole life to this whole art. You have to forget about what other people say. If it's art or anything else, whatever you really, really dig doing, you have to forget about what people say about you sometimes. Forget about this or forget about that. When you're supposed to die or when you're supposed to be living. You have to forget about all these things. You have to go on and be crazy. That's what they call craziness. Craziness is like heaven. Once you reach that point of where you don't give a damn about what everybody else is sayin', you're goin' toward heaven. The more you get into it, they're goin' to say, "Damn, that cat's really flipped out. Oh, he's gone now." But if you producin' and creating, you know, you're gettin' closer to your own heaven. That's what man's trying to get to, anyway.

What's happening is, you, we, we have all these different senses. We've got eyes, nose, you know, hearing, taste and feeling and so forth. Well, there's a sixth sense that's comin' in. Everybody has their own name for it, but I call it Free Soul. And that's more into that mental kind of thing. That's why everything is beyond the eyes now. The eyes only carry you so far out. You have to know how to develop other things that will carry you further and more clear. That's why the fastest speed . . . what's the fastest speed you can think of? They say the speed of light is the fastest thing—that's the eyes— but then there's the speed of thought which is beyond that. You can get on the other side of this theme in a matter of thinking about it, for instance.

Sometimes you might be by yourself writing something. And you come across some words and you just lay back and dig the words and see how that makes you feel. And you might take it at practice or rehearsal or something like that, and get together with it there, in music—see how the music feels. Or either sometimes you might be jamming—when I mean you, I mean the group—the group is jamming or something, and then you might run across something really nice. And then you keep runnin' across that, then you start shoutin' out anything that comes to your mind, you know, whatever the music turns you on to. If it's heavy music, you start singin' things.

Once you have the bottom there you can go anywhere. That's the way I believe. Once you have some type of rhythm, like it can get hypnotic if you keep repeating it over and over again. Most of the people will fall off by about a minute of repeating. You do that say for three or four or even five minutes if you can stand it, and then it releases a certain thing

inside of a person's head. It releases a certain thing in there so you can put anything you want right inside that, you know. So you do that for a minute and all of a sudden you can bring the rhythm down a little bit and then you say what you want to say right into that little gap. It's somethin' to ride with, you know. You have to ride with something. I always like to take people on trips.

That's why music is magic. Already this idea of living today is magic. There's a lot of sacrifices to make. I'm workin' on music to be completely, utterly a magic science, where it's all pure positive. It can't work if it's not positive. The more doubts and negatives you knock out of anything, the heavier it gets and the clearer it gets. And the deeper it gets into whoever's around it. It gets contagious.

Bach and all those cats, they went back in there, and they had caught a whole lot of hell. All they could do was get twenty-seven kids and then dust away. Because the way the society was they didn't

Jimi Hendrix

respect this. They didn't know how to, say, "Well, yeah, he's heavy. We'll go to his concerts. We'll dig him on the personal thing." But like, see, you're not supposed to judge a musician or composer or singer on his personal life. Forget about that. I like Handel and Bach. Handel and Bach is like a homework type of thing. You can't hear it with friends all the time. You have to hear some things by yourself. You can listen to anything that turns you on, that takes you for a ride. People want to be taken somewhere.

I wish they'd had electric guitars in cotton fields back in the good old days. A whole lot of things would have been straightened out. Not just only for the black and white, but I mean for the *cause!*

They keep sayin' things are changing. Ain't nothing changed. Things are going through changes, that's what it is. It's not changes, it's going through changes.

That's the way evolution happens. You have little bumps here. That's why you have the number seven after six. You have six smooth and all of a sudden a little bump. There's gonna be sacrifices. You get a lot of Black Panthers in jail, a lot of—what do you call that war thing?—the moratorium. A lot of those people who are goin' to get screwed up, for instance, here and there. But the whole idea, the whole movement is for everybody to appreciate. It's not only for young people to get it together by the time they're thirty. It's for anybody who's livin' to really appreciate.

It's just like a spaceship. If a spaceship came down, if you know nothin' about it, the first thing you're goin' to think about is shootin' it. In other words, you get negative in the first place already, which is not really the natural way of thinking. But there's so many tight-lipped ideas and laws around, and

Jimi Hendrix

people put themselves in uniform so tightly, that it's almost impossible to break out of that.

Subconsciously what all these people are doing, they're killin' off all these little flashes they have. Like if I told you about a certain dream that was all freaked out, and you'll say, "Oh, wow, you know, where is this at?" That's because you're cuttin' off the idea of wantin' to understand what's in there. You don't have the patience to get into this, and old folks, they think they don't have the patience to do this. They don't have the patience to really check out what's happening through music and what's happening through the theater and science.

It's time for a new national anthem. America is divided into two definite divisions. And this is good for one reason because like somethin' has to happen or else you can just keep on bein' dragged along with the program, which is based upon the past and is always dusty. And the grooviest part about it is not all this old-time thing that you can cop out with. The easy thing to cop out with is sayin' black and white. That's the easiest thing. You can see a black person. But now to get down to the nitty-gritty, it's gettin' to be old and young—not the age, but the way of thinking. Old and new, actually. Not old and young. Old and new because there's so many even older people that took half their lives to reach a certain point that little kids understand now. They don't really get a chance to express themselves. So therefore they grab on to what is happening. That's why you had a lot of people at Woodstock. You can say all the bad things, but why keep elaboratin'? You have to go to the whole balls of it. That's all you can hold on to, in the arts, which is the actual earth, the actual soul of earth. Like writing and sayin' what you think. Gettin' into your own little thing. Doin' this and doin' that. As long as you're off your ass and on your feet some kind of way. Out of the bed and into the street, you know, blah-blah, woof-woof-crackle-crackle—we can tap-dance to that, can't we? That's old hat.

We was in America. We was in America. The stuff was over and starting again. You know, like after death is the end and the beginning. And it's time for another anthem and that's what I'm writin' on now.

Jimi Hendrix

Jimi Hendrix

A Band of Gypsies

Past experience like being around people, jamming—that's the reasons it's being called the Band of Gypsies. Because like I know Jimi has experienced a lot—ten times more than I have. I mean about his playing, about his travels. All of us are people who travel and that's what a gypsy is. A gypsy is a talented person.

Buddy Miles

They can get it together if they want to. The whole world is their front porch.

Musically we try to keep it together. That's why we have to change. That's why personnels in groups always change all the time. 'Cause they're always constantly searching for that certain little thing. The fact of callin' it Gypsies means it could even expand on personnel or so forth and so on. And it's just goin' to be layin' down what we see today. How we see things today. It's no big problem. We have one song in there called "Earth Blues Today." It's nothin' but electronic blues. Electric blues and rock. It's all bottom. It's all rhythm. We're working on our voices. Buddy is gettin' all the voices together where that will be another instrument.

We would like to plan a tour. We'd like to be on the major festivals. We'll play anywhere where we know it's gonna make some kind of penetration or some kind of impact. Anywhere! We can play at the Whiskey, and then we'll play at the Hollywood Bowl. We'll play at all the funky clubs. I mean, we could. We're gearin' ourselves so we could play *anywhere* . . . I might not even be there all the time. Buddy might not even be there all the time, but the core, the whole, the child will be there!

It's nice to try to make yourself into a school. That's what I'd like to get into so I won't be tied down and nobody else will be tied down, because I hate to hang anybody up in any kind of way. That's why everybody will be recognized in anything we get together. You have to go on the cause of it; you can't flash on it.

The sun's going to give you anything and everything you want. The rest is up to you to just go on and dig it.

I'm tired of people usin' the word "love" so much, though. You can mess up a good theme like that. I don't know, we can go on and on and on.

What is perfect? Perfect is death. It's a physical death. Termination.

This is one thing. A lot of people is askin' about why is bright colors come along with rock. I mean is this part of it? It's not hiding. A lot of people say, "Oh, there goes a person with a poster. You know, he's wearin' different posters in his face." You say, "Well, damn, dig it, man, you know somebody's got to be the clown." Which is a magician, for instance. Somebody's got to be this and that. And like, the bright colors, they're always goin' to be there with our music. And sometimes they (the fashion industry) don't want to admit it, but that's what's happened. The young is overtaking. When I mean young is today. Natural thoughts. Just lettin' 'em flow freely.

Jimi Hendrix

A Band of Gypsies

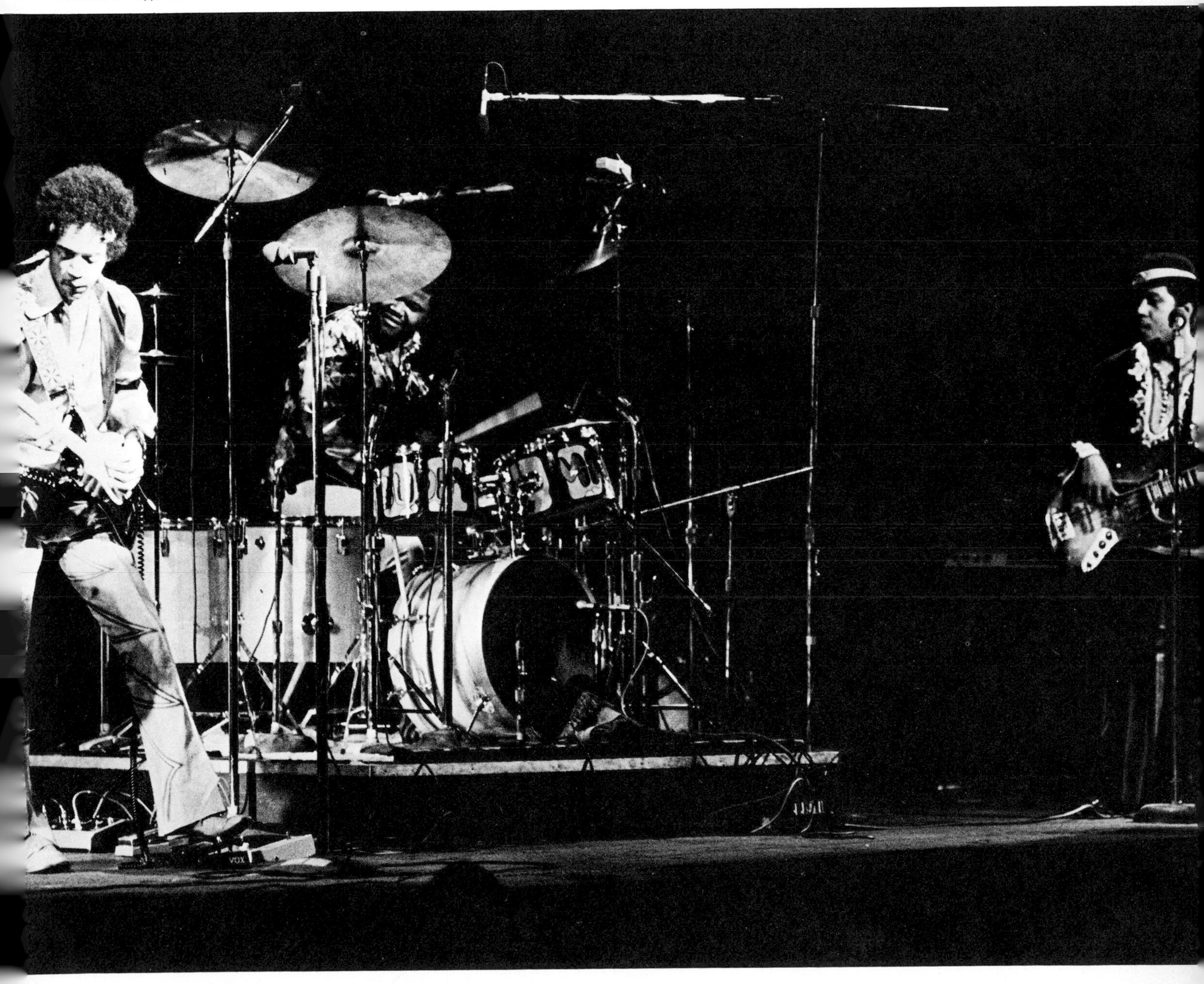

Crosby, Stills, Nash and Young

Right now music somehow inexplicably says, "Yeah, we all like Crosby, Stills, Nash and Young." Right. But why? There's something there about Crosby, Stills, Nash and Young that we all have in common. That, I think, is the next step to explore.

Howard Stein

I've seen Crosby, Stills and Nash burnin' ass. They're groovy. Yeah. Western sky music. All delicate and ding-ding-ding-ding.

Jimi Hendrix

You have a group like Crosby, Stills, Nash and Young that when they walk on the stage, they get a standing ovation before they utter a sound, because they're very good musicians, but they also say hello and they know how to say hello.

Bill Graham

It was no great master plan. It was your usual blind, stoned musicians stumbling around and accidentally falling into a thing of pure. . . . It got us off, and that's what we were lookin' for. It made us feel good. So we kept on doin' it. You know how that is. Very easy.

David Crosby

When they sing acoustically, it's beautiful, man.

Marty Balin/Jefferson Airplane

They've got four voices; they sing right out at top volume, which is the thing that the Hollies and the Byrds used to do terribly well. It's so good, it's so beautiful, it's four voices really coming out strong, but they're very quiet on the verses. But I get the feeling that the real kind of combination is Crosby and Nash. They really sing like they're very, very together, very close together when they're playing.

Adrian Henri/The Liverpool Scene

I knew David very vaguely. As a matter of fact, in his earlier years, I never really liked him too much and had a lot of trouble hanging out with him. He was so harassed and confused by the Byrds and the confusion that businessmen and everybody were putting the Byrds through, as well as the Byrds were putting the Byrds through. But David really began to get delightful, I mean, as he grew and especially after the Byrds because just with that margin of confusion off of his head.

John Sebastian

My last band, by the time it finished, nobody else in it really enjoyed what they were doin'. And I must admit, I didn't either by the time it got to there. I had to get with cats, man, that were turned on by playing, that loved their music. That was basically it. And these cats do.

David Crosby

Crosby, Stills, Nash and Young—that's the Bible!

Audience

There was no concept, man, just mutual bond in music and a mutual attitude about why people should love music if they're going to play music. And Stephen and I both thought we should play it because it got you off, 'cause that's the kind of music we like to play. If it isn't gettin' you off, neither one of us thought that it was too really worthwhile to play.

We'd all already sworn off groups, and we were all gettin' off to our individual careers. Stephen and I were in, like, no more bands, man. Through with it. Forget it. Too many hassles. No deal.

Stephen and I dug each other from afar quite a long time ago when I was still in the Byrds and he was puttin' together the Springfield. He and I had a lot of musical areas in common, most particularly South American and Cuban music, which involves a certain kind of feeling about time. We kind of dug each other, and it grew as we knew each other more. I started writing with him, and I started hanging out with him a lot. And he's crazy. Just as crazy as the rest of us. But at least he's got balls. And genuinely loves music, man. He loves music! He loves it! And that's what I love to be around when I'm playing music.

Stephen was the first one I came to that I wanted to work with. Now, I had known for a long time that I wanted to work with Graham, too, but I didn't know him. I just knew from the Hollies' records that there was one of the best harmony singers in history in there somewhere and I would meet him sooner or later. 'Cause I really thought I was a natural harmony singer. Until I split, I did all the harmony on all the Byrds' records. And he'd just sing rings around me. I think he swallowed a trumpet. Amazing. We call him old razor throat.

One time the Hollies came to L. A. Stephen and the remnants of the nearly defunct Buffalo mush were still there, and he and Neil came down to the Whiskey and I was at the Whiskey, and we watched the Hollies. We all came to the conclusion that, indeed, in the midst of that pile of shit there was the best damn harmony singer around.

So we kind of looked at each other, you know, and we took him home. We got him high, and we talked to him. We rapped and rapped. Really, he's one of the finest cats you're ever likely to meet. On the face of the planet. He's a gentleman. He's got enormous brains, man; he's just really a fine cat. He's somebody you can be proud to walk down anyplace with. He's very brave and equally as gentle. I think he's one of the most highly evolved men I've ever met. And certainly the only gentleman in the band!

David Crosby

God smiled. Greg dropped in our laps. We had been trying to work it out with the old Springfield bass player, but he really is into another form of music. Another instrument. And his head was not really there. We needed somebody that we could truly count on, and you got to understand about bass. It's very big. When you land on a note, you got to really land on it, and it's gotta be really loud. Greg plays his ass off and is just a beautiful person. A really nice cat. He's an incredibly grown-up person to be only nineteen years old. A very, very sweet person and very bright.

David Crosby

All of a sudden it was a real band.

John Sebastian

Neil Young balances out the almost overbearing optimism of Crosby, Stills, and Nash. He is the poet in the group. His songs have an eerie depth. He is the one element that keeps the smooth sound from being slick.

Audience

Steve Stills

We asked John Sebastian to come and be in our band in any capacity. We told John Sebastian that we loved him and his music so much that we didn't care if we had nineteen guitar players, would he please come. And he said, ''You know I want to, but in order to grow I need to be by myself for a while . . . I know what you guys are going to do . . . it's great stuff, 'cause I'd love to. You got what you need.'' He was one of the original Reliability Brothers, anyway. That's a family name. And he can come and play with us any time when we play anyplace, which is good, and he does. We sing his songs and he sings our songs.

David Crosby

David and Graham started singing something together. They started to sing harmonies to each other and it just blew my mind because I'd never known anybody who could sing higher than David. I mean rangewise as well as brainwise. Graham was practically an octave above David. Graham Nash's range is really scary. I think, I'm sure that one of the reasons that he stripped his voice was because he

just has no rules as to "I can't and that's my highest point." I mean, you know, if he can't hit it in his natural voice, which is already as high as my falsetto can ever possibly get, then he goes into a falsetto, you know. So it was just really exciting.

Well, I was sort of the godfather for that band for a while. In the early stages Stephen and Graham and David wanted me to join. At one point they even wanted me to be their drummer, which was pretty amazing because I'm definitely not a drummer. As a matter of fact I sort of discovered Dallas Taylor on the streets of L. A. I met Dallas in a strange way. I'd seen him hanging around Elektra Records for about two days. When I went out to L. A. I was doing a date, a tune called "Baby Don't Ya Get Crazy." I had about eighteen people hired for the session. I was working out with the drummer and rehearsing the rhythm section the day before to give them the feel of the tune I was trying to get. The drummer just didn't get it. It was making me crazy. Dallas had been standing around peeking in and peeking out. I think somebody had already told me once that he was a drummer, but I had, uh, said sort of, "Mmm, yeah, that's nice," you know. So finally this other guy left the room for a minute, and I was sort of walking around going, "Oh, God, what can I do?" and Dallas comes over and says, "Hey, man, I think I can play that." So I said, "Really? Oh, great, man," you know, "sit down." So I started to play the tune. Well, Dallas just completely curled my hair. I mean, he's—to this day—my very favorite drummer for the kind of areas that I get into. He hears time the most like me of anybody that I've met yet. Dallas ended up doing my entire album. I was thinking of using Dallas, and I was sort of tentatively, at that time, also thinking of maybe getting a little band together to work for me. But the truth of the matter was that I wasn't really ready for that yet. I was a little bit too hung up to be able to commit myself to Dallas.

So Dallas came out to Sag Harbor and so did Stephen and Graham and David and in fact so did Harvey Brooks and Paul Harris. And there was a couple of weeks when that was going to be the band. But it just didn't gel. Without any bad feelings or anything, that formation disbanded. Meanwhile, Graham, David, and Stephen had still been getting it on vocally and learning tunes and so on and so on. It was really one of the longest band pregnancies of all times. It was scaring me to death because I

Graham Nash and David Crosby

was saying, "Oh, they're blowin' it. They're gonna just take too much time," and so on. The first time that I really had a chance to listen to them pick a whole set was at the Greek Theater in L. A. I went every night to see how consistent it was, how together they were, and I came away from that week at the Greek Theater just "yeaing" because they were a band.

David says that he feels like they all joined Greg Reeves, and not like Greg Reeves joined their band, 'cause Greg is an unbelievable bass player. He's twenty; he's put in all these dues; it's ridiculous. You know, like between him and Dallas, it's like the juvenile delinquents, you know. They've already put in all these dues and they're only nineteen, twenty years old and have got it so together. Greg did all that stuff; he did "Cloud Nine" with the Temptations; he recorded with Aretha, I think, and was a Motown studio man for three years.

John Sebastian

San Francisco—
Jefferson Airplane and
Creedence Clearwater Revival

The San Francisco bands happened just as things had started dying—when it wasn't English rock groups one after another. Then all of a sudden San Francisco happened and gave it all that new boost and new life.

Audience

The bands are not the priesthood. They're part of the community. They're an essential part. They're the joymakers. They do it. And they got to get off and play good, man, and make people feel like boogiein' and laughin' and playin'. That's their gig; they communicate. But they're not the essential thing. They were not what was happening there. It's a good thing. It's part of the signals. It's the music and the freedom and the freedom from paranoia most specifically in that case. And I think that everybody there was higher on one other thing than anything else. They were higher on seeing that their value system worked. This value system, this revolution, man, in essence is a revolution in values and ethics, which, of course, is something that mistakenly is not defended. You see, they're fools. Values and ethics are the exact core of human thought. They're what matters to you. And we have changed those—drastically. The percentages of young people who are buying the old value systems have gone from say eighty percent to about twenty percent and the rest of 'em are buying ours. We offered them an alternative. Laugh. Groove. Get high. Ball. Create. Grow. Learn. Change. Birth. The other way just stood no chance in a child's mind to that. Any child could see the truth, man, if he hasn't been messed

up already. But they have a truth sense that far surpasses intellectuality. They know that we're doing something that's closer to a human way, you dig? They sense that instantly. Intellectually, half of 'em couldn't tell you. But they can feel, most definitely, that they are getting off more and that you are supposed to be happy. You dig it? For me, it's a transference from the old Judeo-Christian "you are supposed to be unhappy, and if you work at it, we might give you a little bit of happiness someday, but you better be nice now!" That whole ethic is bullshit. It's rooted in suppression and control and manipulatory games of people who twisted an original truth.

David Crosby/Crosby, Stills, Nash and Young

Not being snobby about it, but like San Francisco's really a small city and there's water on all sides. It can't get any bigger. And so it's pretty. It's like a small town. You know more about what's going on, say, than a person in New York knows about what's

Grace, Paul and Jorma

32

Jefferson Airplane

going on in New York. There's millions of things going on, like music, like fifteen different clubs going on every night of the week—Mondays, Sundays—and you can go and hear bands, new bands, all the time. It doesn't really happen much outside San Francisco.

It's a good city. The police and the people sometimes they get tough, but they don't hassle too much. There's not a big political machine there. There's nothing big in San Francisco. There's no big business trip, there's no like organized crime, big syndicate-type trip or anything. It's like a lot of little things going on in a small area. There's not enough room for any one of them to get big, because that means eight people will get shoved out here, and they get pissed off.

We like to play outdoors. True, it's San Francisco, not just us. Everybody in San Francisco did it; it's not our thing. We just happen to be the ones that got out more and did it outside, too. The Grateful Dead used to do it all the time and still do. Everybody does, Steve Miller, Quicksilver, Sons of Champlin, Santana. Almost all the bands.

People attract themselves, also. It's not just the music. The music is just something to focus on. Like in the park in San Francisco. People don't come to the park just to go out and sit and hear a band—like they go to the Fillmore or like they came to Shea Stadium when the Beatles were there. They come out to go out to the park. A lot of people used to go out for a picnic. You go out and meet a lot of your friends; you find people you haven't seen for a long time. Sit in the sunshine. Take your clothes off. Smoke dope. Hear bands playing for a while. You can walk off in the trees, come back later, and there's another band playing. You can eat. There's no audience-band thing. Just a get-together in the park. Just go out in the park. Everybody does what they like to do. Some people like to play music. Some people like to sit around and get high. Some people like to ride motorcycles around the park. Bring their children, and it works out. Everybody enjoys themselves. Some guys feel like they want to play on the stage, they start bands, and a couple of weeks later, months later they're up there playing.

Paul Kantner

The Jefferson Airplane and the Grateful Dead and us have proceeded along the path together. For instance, we're playing with the Grateful Dead in New York this weekend. Well, three years ago we were playing with the Grateful Dead in Napa, California, for two hundred bucks apiece for each band. So we started from the bottom together and we're sort of all along the line, playing the same places. I know the life they live because we show up two weeks before or two weeks after. They get through playing in the same club or in the same hotel or the same airline. It's really the same life. Stylistically we are related. In being from the Bay Area and coming together at about the same time under very similar conditions and taking the same drugs. I don't know if it's acid rock. It's Bay Area music. I mean we started out in the same halls, playing with those people a great deal. And if you listen, all the bands from the Bay Area have a similarity in sound. They're all related in some respects. And not only that, but we've all heard each other so much that we've all influenced each other. The vocalists are different. And the lyric trip may be different. It's a blues form, I guess, extending into raga music at times. It's loud. It has a certain amount of power, and it flows a certain way in a jam session. The last night that Jack played with us at a performance at the Fillmore, we had Jack on stage, Mickey Hart from the Grateful Dead, Jorma Kaukonen, Jerry Garcia, and Steve Miller and myself and the rest of the band all playing together, and it all made sense. Everybody knew how to play with each other. All those people had never played together on the same stage before.

There's something about that music. It's like blues musicians don't have to know each other to get together to play. Well, this music isn't blues, but there is a way of playing, and it's very free. It's actually quite free, but it's based on certain ideas and a lot of cooperation. We all sort of fell under the same set of circumstances, coming from San Francisco in the beginning, sharing the same sort of idealism, playing for free, playing in the parks a lot. Dropping a lot of acid. Psychedelics. Owsley is close to all those bands. Or was close to all those bands. The changes came later. What's happened to us and to the Jefferson Airplane has really been a very similar trip. The only difference being that the home base is ten miles apart, across the bay. We've both enjoyed a certain degree of success, perhaps even more so than the Grateful Dead. We've played the same circuit. And home is the same place.

Barry Melton/Country Joe & the Fish

We didn't get paid for a long time when we started. It just set a trend, you see. It was also somethin' to do on an afternoon, to go out to the park and play. Had a good time. Smoked a lot of dope and just generally got it on. People come and listen to music and hang out. When they're good, they're just really nice. Nice and soothing. If it's warm enough for us to move our fingers, we usually like to play. You'll see us pissed off when it's cold out there! I just feel like, hey, man, there's a place to set up and play and a bunch of people'll come and everybody'll jump up and down. And if not, they can split and go home and watch TV or go off in their car or somethin' or whatever. When we played Hawaii we did a free concert. And as it turned out, it probably was the first decent-sized free concert that they had. I couldn't believe it. It was so warm. One would think that they would have 'em all the time. It'd give the bands a chance to play and people could hear 'em. They just hadn't thought of it. I, personally, don't usually think of it. Paul will think of it and say, "Hey, how would you like to do a concert on Sunday?" And we'll have just worked Saturday night, and I might say, "Oh, man, we've just worked." But everybody shows up when we do it anyway because, yeah, it's a good idea. We'll go do it. And we'll have fun. They almost always are.

Jack Casady and Jorma Kaukonen

Grace, Paul and Jorma

Jefferson Airplane

People in this band have quit for the last three years, myself included. Maybe I even hold the record. It's just the thing of somehow realizing that it's just not that important, man, and that we all kind of like each other as much as we argue and as much as we have differences of opinion. We all like each other and we still sort of hang together. I think it's because it's the only life we know. We've been doing it for four years and I think about, you know, gee, I'd like to have either my own band, or record my own album, or be a producer and take on other groups, but when I start thinking about people I'd like to use, it runs down to people in this band. We're very close friends. And I think that what's happening is that that's getting done. Right now the other half of our band is on with two other people. So we're spreading out. Plus for some reason there's security here. We're all on salary and I can't imagine anybody wanting to go to the band and not finding their weekly check there. It's run just like a corporation. The money goes in one account and we pay ourselves out of it. And we can't overspend, etcetera, blah-blah. The opportunities are limitless for having just a name like Jefferson Airplane. I think eventually we will be getting into films. Not maybe everybody together, but certain members. And we'll be getting into solo and single albums and we'll maybe be doing some writing. Maybe of books, maybe of music.

Also recording with friends. For instance the last album, both David Crosby and Stephen Stills helped us with that. Plus a multitude of other people. Cass included. I don't know how many people are on the payroll, but it's probably twenty or some odd number like that, not including people that are our lawyers that we have to send monthly checks to, and PR firms, and you know all that stuff that has to keep it going. 'Cause there's so many people involved and everybody benefits, and nobody loses. If they feel like they do, they usually come out and air their problems, one way or another, and we all rap at each other for a long period of time, and we get over that hump.

Spencer Dryden

There's no such thing as anybody's band. A bunch of people working together always dictates that it doesn't come out the way you think it's going to in front. But in a lot of ways it's more rigid. When it's working right, we play more rigidly, and you play more parts 'cause you're trying. Bluntly, it's not as subtle. You're trying to get things together for a more forceful effect when it works. Preferably to get people dancing. Well, see, the thing is, it doesn't really matter, but if it gets people moving, they ought to be able to get up and dance. Ideally, the concert hall situation isn't ideal. By and large, you know, we're not a show band so we can't often just turn on our dynamics. And if there're other people moving around, it helps. You can play off the audience. A lot of bands have it down so they can just turn themselves on "click" and straight ahead. But like our, or my own personal approach—I find that I really play a lot off the response that's happening. If I can establish some sort of rapport, it's easier to get off. Yeah, that's about right. You can be anyplace. We've played the strangest halls in the strangest little towns that have gotten it on very well. We played in Columbus not too long ago, and everybody got off solidly. It blew my mind, you know, Columbus, Ohio. The all-American city. A fine show.

Jorma Kaukonen

I'm very big into soul music. That's my trip. I really dig it. I grew up in it. Then I got sidetracked into folk, and then the Airplane, and now I'm gettin' back to the nitty-gritty. I really dig soul.

The thing about black music is that it's positive, you know. White music is frustrated and drugged up and just doesn't have any faith. It really doesn't have, man, they don't have any faith. You know what I mean? People come to listen to rock and roll because that's their religion. And yet they don't know how to believe. They don't know how to let go. And the police are subversive enough that they stop it. But the black people are free. And that's really where it's at.

I can dig it, man, 'cause they got a lot to say. They got somethin' to say and they got a lot of faith and they got a lot of belief. A lot of white people don't have that faith, you know. Or they got such a tiny faith. And they have no release. And black people got a release.

Marty Balin

Grace

36

I think Jack Casady is the world's greatest electric bass player. Jack plays all over the instrument; he plays music on it instead of just bass lines. Like a lot of bass players will just play bass lines over and over again, but Jack will play along with the guitar player or along with the drummer, and he'll make a whole musical line out of his bass line. And not only that, he gets the quintessence of the Fender bass kind of sound. He's the master of that style of bass playing. He's the most evolved product of rock and roll bass playing. Actually, even in jazz, they don't play the bass like that. Although it seems his playing is evolved a lot from jazz bass players, it seems to me that his stuff is more highly evolved than any jazz bass player's stuff, if only because he just puts it in there. He doesn't wait for a solo to do something and just play a pattern the rest of the time.

Phil Lesh/The Grateful Dead

Casady plays a sort of French horn lead line that's just stupendous. Unbelievable.

David Crosby/Crosby, Stills, Nash and Young

Paul's a revolutionary. I mean, he really is. Some people have a lot of politics. Some people have politics in their music. Like Paul's politics comes out in his music and he's really beautiful for what he's doin'. And I admire what he does, but I can't do that. I can't do that. To me music is always just love, I guess, just happiness. Singin' a happy song. I don't think politics should enter into music. When it does, it makes me a little queasy. 'Cause I don't dig politics that much.

Marty Balin

Jack Casady is a very particular person and very meticulous about his playing and his setup; it involved more for the road staff than it did for me. For instance, he wouldn't play out of his cabinets until they were tuned to a perfect studio A, 440 A, and he would tilt them until they were absolutely correct.

Barry Melton/Country Joe & the Fish

There's gotta be balance. Certain people have to be the stability. Certain people have to be the freakness. Certain people have to be uncontrollable and grab but that's what makes it go forward, see. They're out there taking the knob.

It's just like life: there's things you don't want to touch on and things that get ugly, but people are upset and hurt.

People speak their minds at times when they don't have their minds totally with them. They'll say things I think they don't mean. And it'll hurt, and maybe the whole band will be affected by just two people arguing. We've been on the road three weeks, and something went down last week and just like a whole lot of little things, and nobody could even be with each other. And it was bad. I mean, it was 'cause problems like in between groups within the band. But all of a sudden people realized maybe what they've said or done to affect another one, because they feel it themselves, and they'll come out and they'll say, "Hey, man, I'm sorry." They come out. Because they want to be friends. Everybody wants good. Nobody wants anything bad, man, nobody wants bad vibes or not getting along. Paul'll give you gifts. He gave me a funny tie once, and he didn't have to do anything else. It was like a week after we'd had a very bad argument. I just smiled. In other words, he's got the feelings. All the feelings are there. I think he's right, too. He's the one outer strength the band has. He's the one thing that holds everything together. If it weren't for Paul, there would be no Jefferson Airplane. He wants it so badly, and he makes you do the things to put it together. And I've seen arguments, bad ones, I mean, things where the tension in the room is so great you want to run outside and scream or take a drive. It gets on a level, man—it's like a twenty-four-hour Synanon. They're very frank and out-front about it. I think that that's what a lot of bands don't understand. A lot of bands also go too fast. I think that's why Crosby, Stills, etcetera, etcetera, are taking their time. For instance, they took a long time before they played their first time. And they're taking a long time making their second album. A long time with the interviews and things. And I think they're doing it—because they're all professionals. They've all been in bands before, and they know what that scene is like. And they're learning how to get in step. Growing. They're growing a family.

Spencer Dryden

We've already won our revolution. I mean, we're doing what we want to do within a context that doesn't cause any hassles. And that's what you basically revolt about; I mean, you're uncomfortable. But running out in the street is sort of senseless. Unless you want to get your head beat in.

Paul Kantner

All the words don't necessarily mean that. They're not necessarily dictations, you know, like the Five-Step Plan to go out for a revolution or something. They're just thoughts that run through a songwriter's head, too. And they're not seriously taken verbatim and so on.

Can't spell it out much more than that. Can't run around and try and interpret every word, you know. It's like the way people tear apart lyrics to various songs. They'll make anything that they feel like that they are. If a guy feels like goin' out and killin' a guy, he'll say, "That song 'Revolution' made me go out and kill a guy." And if a guy feels like balling some chick, then he'll say, "That song made me feel like I wanted to ball a chick."

It doesn't imply a bloodbath. It's a thing about change. There's a lot of ways to get it through. It's makin' people think about it. I mean, that's what it's all about. That's what everybody does, whether it's a news commentator or a teacher writing a book. He's looking for followers because he believes something.

Paul is saying something, and you hear the words. If you're playing along, like I can't play a tune well if the words embarrass me, or I can't get some sort of content from 'em, see. So what I'm doing implies a tacit approval, but I'm not verbal about it. You wouldn't find me on a soapbox, but I have found Paul on one. He says it and we sort of kick him along.

He's a songwriter. He writes songs, usually with the idea of the word content first and then the music, see. So the emphasis tends to fall a lot of times on the words.

Various members of the band have rejected various different songs for the reason that they just didn't dig 'em. They didn't believe 'em, or they just couldn't do 'em. So, if we do a thing, and keep doing it for any length of time, it implies that people are pretty well behind it. Otherwise they get junked. If we can't play 'em good, they get junked.

Jack Casady and Jorma Kaukonen

The Airplane's a structured thing with three voices, and you play a lot of different parts and structured things in order to make the total come out.

Jack Casady

Paul knows the words to say. He's got a good choice of words. Sometimes they aren't always good, but, man, they'll get a reaction. He used to be, like, in high school, he used to be debate team captain. He used to be boxing champion. So that cat's got both the physical and mental front going.

Spencer Dryden

It's not necessarily about the revolutionary movement. It's about what's going on.

Paul Kantner

Revolution? Let's put it this way: change is imminent, or a need for change is imminent. We're right in there pitching. Well, what can I say? I wouldn't mind kickin' a cop in the ass. Paul formulates those ideas, and I react to 'em! Like when I get hassled, I'll get up-tight. Most of the time my genteel upbringing keeps me in line. Like, you'll notice that I haven't written a "revolution" song. But I do play 'em. The idea sounds all right to me. I'm for it. Why not? You see, my heart's with him.

Jorma Kaukonen

Jorma finds the ethnic heroes, man, he finds 'em on the street. He's young, see. He's a young man, and he's feelin' it. I can dig that.

Spencer Dryden

Grace Slick is one of the strongest negative factors this side of the Rolling Stones. She and Paul are both pretty cynical, powerful, and dominating. This doesn't mean she's not good—she's terrific. She's developed this fantastic electric guitar voice!

Audience

Jack, Jorma and Marty

Creedence Clearwater Revival

We play rock and roll. We don't go any deeper than that ever.

We've been together for a lot of years, and we want people to see the group as a group first. And we're still in that stage. Nobody knows much about us really, except that we've been together for nineteen zillion years and where'd you get your funny name.

I couldn't imagine the band breaking up, taking on a replacement. We fooled around with other musicians through the years, especially me. I went out and played for money, 'cause none of us was making anything. The band never broke up. We'd just go on little vacations. There was never even a question of the band breaking up. Even though I played like for months with another group. It was really like getting through that period so that we could get back together again.

We used to call ourselves a blues band, even though we weren't really very bluesy. It was 'cause we didn't have the instruments. We had piano, drums, and guitar. It's hard to get away from the sameness of it all with just those instruments. We didn't have horns or bass or anything, so it was just tinky-tink all the time. We played blues, not white blues, really. We played more rock and roll blues. We did some very lyrical stuff, even when we were forging it together. Again, about what we do now: it was blues influenced, but it wasn't really blues per se. We didn't copy strict formats for a blues song. We just sort of took the twelve-bar blues and went with it. But we do a lot of things that you just don't do. We play a lot prettier than you're supposed to, and that sort of thing. That's just the way it came out.

That's the only part of the blues interest revival that we like. Most of it we don't like because people are liking the wrong blues artists. They're liking the watered-down versions. That's why we refuse to even try to be in the same arena with that, 'cause we aren't. We don't want to be, 'cause, I mean, it would be a sacrilege to try and compete with Howlin' Wolf. Financially, sure, we'd knock 'em dead. I don't know what it is, but their time is over, really. Howlin' Wolf's a little too old to be caught up in the thing, 'cause he's not going to come up with anything new, I don't think. But during his time I thought he was tops. In those days your reward was like three beers and maybe a week at the Sportsmen's Club. That was about all you got.

John Fogerty

I think Fogerty is one of the greatest writers going today. I nearly fell out of a car the first time I heard "Lodi." Killed me because I mean it was really, it was a song. It was right down my alley because it was just talk and talk.

Somehow the top half of the neck has fascinated more guitarists these days than any other area on the instrument. Fogerty plays them chords, man. He plays 'em just right! He's got a great hand. I can't help but like him.

John Sebastian

We used to really get up-tight about being called another San Francisco band. I did especially. I sure did. 'Cause I knew where we were going, and I knew we had the right ideas, and I just kind of knew everything was going to fall together, and I hated people putting the brand names on before I even got a chance to do anything. Etcetera, etcetera, ad nauseam. Like now, it's nice to know that way back before we made it, I can look at this thing and say, "Gee, I really had to fight for that, but I knew it was a success." Not afterward, where you have pretty much a good chance of getting a song played anyway. Like the way it is now. We did a lot of things before we made it that we're using now. For us it's gratifying to know that we were on the right track.

We didn't see much future in the psychedelic stuff. Some of it I really liked. That's a bad term to use; call it progressive music, okay. But they hit one level, like it took maybe five years to get it all together, to get enough songs to make a good album

John Fogerty

40

of progressive rock. And then that was the end. It'll take another five years to get enough together to make another good one. So we didn't see much future as a working kind of idiom of music in that kind of thing. That was the big vogue, and so much of it was crap. We'd go hear the bands. We'd hear maybe one good song, one good lick from the guitar player in twenty minutes of playing. It's like he's searching for it, and then he'd find it, and we'd all go, "Yeah! He found it!" And then it'd be another twenty minutes. . . .

Well, syntax is really involved there. Semantics. 'Cause that's supposed, from where we sit, anyway, that's supposed to be the professional musician, the guy who can sit and ad-lib or—what's the other word besides ad-lib?—improvise. Right. And like those have good connotations, like wow—yeah—he's really into it; he's ad-libbing or he's improvising! But people don't really realize that most of these improvisations—the good ones—are memory, and the bad ones are he's got no idea where he's going. He's playing and then he thinks about what he did

after. And somebody who is really going to ad-lib knows what he's going to do before he plays it. It didn't occur to him ten minutes ago. He's played around that sort of thing; he knows his scales; he knows his instrument. And most people that are doing it now don't know their instrument. Really, that's why Benny Goodman—seems like a name out of nowhere—but that era, those people knew their instruments. They studied their music, maybe for twenty years. Most of 'em were a little older, too, when they started making it. And when they sat down to improvise, they knew where they were going in their heads before they started playing a bunch of notes. I mean, they were writing a good solo right there, and they knew exactly what it was going to sound like, even though they were just making it up.

Nowadays guys are just playing on a string to see what it will sound like. Rather than a conscious effort. And that's really the difference. You know, we really improvise a lot, but it sounds finished. When I improvise, if it doesn't sound finished, then

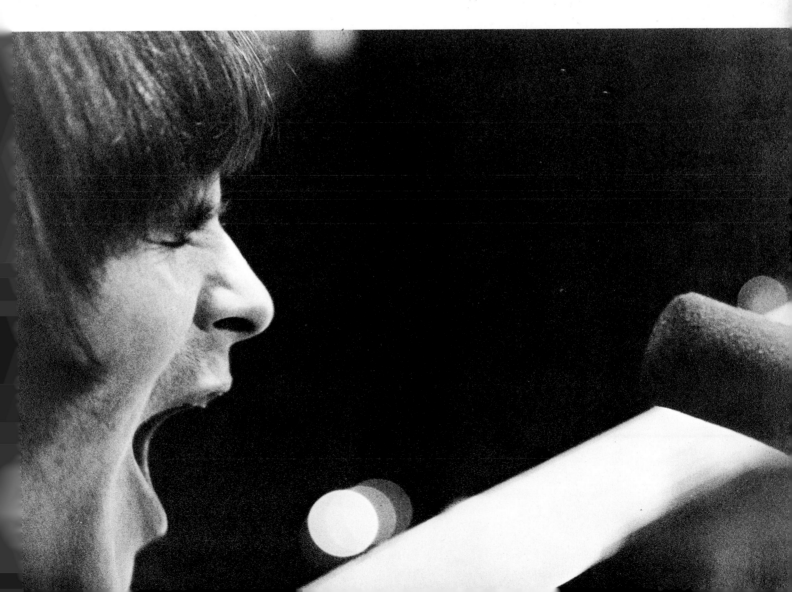

Stu Cook

it's out and out bad. Like I'll just shake my head and stop, 'cause it ain't makin' it. But I'd say nine times out of ten, when I improvise, it works out 'cause I'm thinking about it before I do it. But the audience, or critics or whatever, they think I'm playing note for note what's on the record. I'm not. But it sounds finished, so they say, ''Ah ha! He's playin' the same solo.'' And that ain't what's happenin' at all. Eventually, maybe ten years from now, somebody'll figure that one out! We improvise a lot, even on our records.

John Fogerty

I love their record. They're good. It's real rock and roll. It's cool. It just creates a feeling, and it does that well. It's just happy, good-time music. They never deviate at all. They're on the other end of the spectrum. I appreciate me for what I do and appreciate them for what they do.

Johnny Winter

We practice weekdays. Take the weekend off just like the plumbers. What should I say? It gives us a mission in life.

It isn't all work. Actually it isn't work anyway. Sometimes it is. It depends on the song. When I say work I mean it's challenging. But we enjoy it anyway. That's what it's all about really. Otherwise I guess most people die when they're about four. That's about all they can take. Like sometimes we're working specifically on a song or an album or a group of songs, and other times we have a couple of months where we're really not working on anything. We're just playing. And that helps bring back things maybe we've forgotten about for a while. Like they both have their value. It's fun to finally finish an album and get it done, you know. Then it's committed to history, so to speak. You don't have to worry about it anymore. Sometimes we have to learn the songs all over again if we're going to play them in person. It's like studying for an exam, really.

Doug Clifford

Pshew! and it's gone. It covers the whole thing as a musician. Like we do it ideally. Like we think every musician should really. Part of it is work, and part of it is playing just to hear the notes come out.

My vocal style came mainly from not having a P.A. system loud enough to carry the voice, so I always had to put the songs in a key high enough that they could be heard above the music. And after shouting and shouting—it was mostly like playing a game of football on Saturday afternoon. Songs were just loud, like I was shouting across a football field. From that a power sort of had to develop. It was either that or get laryngitis. In the beginning I used to, but it was mostly because I was trying too hard. I didn't really know what it was, you know, how to control it. I'd use all the air, everything'd just come out. But you don't have to do that to get the sound you want.

I like that tape-delay echo a lot. In recording I use my voice like an instrument. It's another sound apart from the way my voice sounds. It's a thing that was used a lot on kind of the country rock and roll records of the fifties. But it isn't because we're trying to revive old rock and roll or anything. It just happened to be something I liked. It was a good idea. And it's still a good idea, put it that way, and I still like it.

It is hard to make a band work. 'Specially when things are good rather than 'specially when things are bad. 'Cause the pressure that's put on you or that people will try to lay on you, let's say, is almost insurmountable. If you're lucky you figure it out before you break up. You just say, "Wow! All this pressure is just twisting. It's like a reflection in a funny mirror, it's just going . . . tcheeoo!" Everything gets all distorted. And if you get into it too far you don't realize that all it is is the pressure doing that to you. Nothing's really any different. And most bands break up, and they hate each other at the end, and they don't realize that nobody changed, that it's just their view of things. Anyway, finally you just tell all of the people that are laying it on, like those agents, and those press agents, and those promoters, and relatives with their ideas of what you should do. You just tell 'em all, "Get lost! You weren't around when we were struggling, and now we've made it." You figure out that you and you alone knew what you were doing to get where you got. Let me go back and do what I always wanted to do anyway. That's really the hardest part of the whole thing. You become like the center of your little universe.

John Fogerty

Tom Fogerty

The Performers

FOLK/COUNTRY ROCK

Somebody asked me a year ago if country music was going to be a big thing. I always thought it was a big thing.

Felix Pappalardi/Mountain

Country music has been big for a long time. It's just that other people are getting into it now. And realizing the value of it, and it's a beautiful form. We have a tune that's called "Big Bird." It has a country feel to it. We didn't write it to be a country tune. It just happened to be a country tune. We don't like to put labels. It's just an indication that we aren't really into writing a rock and roll song and a country song and this one's going to be classically oriented. . . . But like this country tune, which it turned out to be, for instance, has in the middle of it, there is somewhat of a bridge that's in six-eight. Tom Webb, our sax player, just improvises against a jazzy kind of rhythm thing and then he goes tenor and I take over on violin, the same type of thing, and then boom, "Big Bird." It's back in country again.

Jerry Goodman/The Flock

See, Ray Charles hipped a lot of the black people to the country and western bands. Where before they weren't hip about us, like we was kind of listening before, but still he made it just even more down-to-earth where you could dig it. And then if you pay attention to a lot of these country and western things, they are out of sight.

The lyrics are really involved, but it's not only a deep story. It's written so plain the average layman can understand it. Like they say, "I went down the street and I picked up a cigarette butt." Anybody can understand it, "I went down the street and picked up a cigarette butt." And that's just the way they write. It's just as clear. And you can understand their stories. But they are involved now. The stories are really about everyday happenings and stuff. And then a lot of the tunes, a lot of the melodies that they put to these songs will make tearjerkers.

That's why a lot of the blues singers dig it, because blues is tellin' what's happening like around you.

Man, I've heard some country and western tunes, like, really after you sit down and listen to it, it makes you feel funny inside, just like seein' a movie or something. You know how some movies can get to you? Hey, I've heard tunes like that, country and western, that have got to me the same. . . .

Gladys Knight and the Pips

Whew! My God! Country and western music is beautiful. It's been around a long time. I tell you who I used to be crazy about: Roger Miller. There's a nut, man. That cat, man. I used to turn on the radio to hear a tune called "My Uncle Used to Love Me But She Died."

Wilson Pickett

There's been a lot of guys that are playing rock and roll that were kind of at the same place I was, that is, playin' folk music, country music, old-time music, some kind of noncommercial music, that normally urban white kids weren't into. Then when the huge pop thing, the Beatles, and everything started coming out, a lot of those guys went over to electric music, just like I did. And now after having built up reputations for themselves in these various groups, many of them are choosing to play the kind of music that they were playing before, just for the hell of it. Like, the Byrds, Poco, Flying Burrito Brothers, and others. . . . The Band is almost a country band.

A lot of it is approach rather than actual sound or actual musical material. Most of it can be in the lyrics, even. You notice the textural change immediately. And that's the change that you associate with country music. Country music is as homogeneous as rock and roll is. The blues, spade music, soul music, is the same way. I mean everybody's coppin' freely from each other. Aretha Franklin does "The Weight"; Flatt and Scruggs do Bob Dylan songs.

Jerry Garcia/The Grateful Dead

The Who

The Byrds

I mean we're only influenced a little bit by blue-grass because I used to play it. I wouldn't say we're still playing bluegrass. It fits perfectly with Byrd songs, anything we do. The Byrds have always sounded a little country, anyways, in bluegrass.

Clarence White

It's about the only group around that's still playing electric twelve-string. Paul McCartney at one time was very concerned about our career and he wrote us a letter saying that we had to drop the Byrd glasses and the twelve-string. No alternatives suggested. Merely just get rid of them. A very cryptic note actually.

Roger McGuinn

I knew Jimmy (now Roger) McGuinn in the folk days when he was working at the Playhouse singing Beatle tunes with a twelve-string guitar and really puzzling all the ethnic folk musicians who were standing around saying, "Goodness, this doesn't go with, fit all the rules and regulations that we've carefully evolved for traditional music."

John Sebastian

How did I decide to form the Byrds? I saw the Beatles, that's why. Bang. That's the answer. That's all. That was enough. It turned me on, you know. I wanted to get a four-piece or five-piece group together with electric instruments and try to do that because it looked like a lot of fun. The same reason that everybody else is ganging into it, you know. I don't blame them. I'm just saying it's a phenomenon. It's happening. It will eventually cause the demise of the style.

Roger McGuinn

The Grateful Dead

I have had an interest in country music generally because I used to play bluegrass music, and before that I was in traditional—old-time—band music, and before that old-time ballads and the traditional styles performing them, and that was the thing that I was into just before I got into rock and roll, electric music, electric instruments. The stuff I liked about that kind of music, I still like about it. . . . It's just selecting what you like, and one of the things I liked about it was the pedal steel guitar, because of the fact that it's an electric instrument and a recent instrument, and it seemed to have a lot of possibilities to me. I thought I would try and take it on.

Jerry Garcia

The Dead are one of the finest families there is anywhere of any kind. They're just chock-full of some really superb people, man, hugely creative and really bright and totally human and very honest and very funky and very straight. I really love them very deeply. They're good people.

David Crosby/Crosby, Stills, Nash and Young

That was just always where we felt music should be. I came to this music from a whole other place than where Jerry came, but it was equally stylized. I had had a little jazz experience, and although that idiom didn't appeal to me, and a contact with Indian music also—all these things in combination with whatever is the improvisatory spirit would make the music of the future, whatever that is! And now here it is. Music is pretty much like that.

We were one of the first ones to be deafening! Electric instruments can be played, you can get more expressive nuances, like dynamically, out of electric instruments than anybody ever could out of any other instruments, so it's possible to play just as soft on electric instruments as it is on a normal instrument. But on the other hand, you can go ten times as loud. But the trouble is that you kind of tend to get in the groove of loud and stay there. So dynamics are really hard to do.

Phil Lesh

Jerry Garcia

And sometimes there's a dynamic scale, all of which is at least above the level of really bein' loud, so it's like you don't really perceive it . . .

Jerry Garcia

. . . as loudness. You sometimes perceive it as weight on different parts of your body, on your heart or on your lungs, on the back of your neck. Sometimes bass players can walk right up and down my spine. It depends on where you are in a hall, that sort of thing, but electric instruments work on that level, too. And at the same time, of course, it's deafening. I kind of think that people tend to shut that off. The part that's deafening. Even though my hearing seems to have declined, I can still perceive things, although they tend to be loud, the things that I perceive.

Phil Lesh

It's another dimension.

Jerry Garcia

The Byrds

Country Joe & the Fish

A rock and roll band is in a sense a political force. So you just try to communicate those things that we believe, our way of life. I don't know—just the joy, doin' somethin' together, people dancin', having a good time together, sharing a common experience. That's our politics.

I believe that I come from a school of musicians from a certain place and a certain time, and that any of us can communicate with each other. I play a certain kind of music from a certain place. Actually, the whole West Coast. I played with the Canned Heat. Bear sang with our band before on one occasion. People from the West Coast, California, strange, but there is a communication involved there.

We started out as small-town boys from Berkeley, which is a kind of small town where you're very politically oriented. Both Joe and I came from parents who were leftists (I don't know if they are now). Berkeley was sort of a logical place to go, and in Berkeley you demonstrate a lot. That used to be the major form of social communication. I'm talking

about the days before rock halls, even. If you wanted to meet a girl or play music or talk or whatever, you went out to one of those demonstrations where there were a thousand young people out there singing together and having a good time. I mean demonstrations turned into a bad time, but when we started out in Berkeley, they were a good time. Nothing serious ever happened. No violence or anything. They were pleasant street experiences where people sang together and protested about Mississippi two thousand miles from it, you know.

At any rate, you think you know stuff. You think you know about world situations until you start traveling a lot. I think we travel more than the president. He ought to be forced to travel as much as we are. When you start traveling a lot you start seeing, well, you realize that it's all beyond your comprehension. The fact that somebody can be the president of the United States, after all I've traveled, amazes me. Because I don't understand it at all. And I'm moving all over at an incredible rate of speed every year. Over a quarter of a million miles a year. I travel mostly in this country. The more I travel, the less I understand. I mean, really complex—from city to city, and person to person. And when you live in one place, it's easy to have definite ideas like that. When you start traveling a lot, it's really hard, and so that's what happened to our politics. It got spaced out. The more you travel, the less you know, and the more tolerant you become. Even the people I used to hate in the past. And some of the people I used to respect in the past and really think they were wise, and all that stuff.

Another thing that happened when we got famous, we got a chance to meet all those underground political leaders and heroes that we'd always had. They were the voices over the microphones at the demonstrations. You never really knew. When you meet them and find out that they're just people, and they don't know what the hell's going on, then your trust and all that stuff is eradicated. So the only politics that we do now is our own politics.

Barry Melton

Country Joe

John Sebastian

John Sebastian

While I was quote studying at NYU unquote I wasn't really studying at NYU. What I was doing was sleeping through most of my classes, leaving early, cutting a few more classes, and going over to Tom Veechguara's little guitar shop on Fourth Street on the East Side and building classical guitars. I was just his apprentice. I worked for a year and a half. At the end of the year and a half, I had grown enough into it that I could build my own instrument. And I built myself a beautiful classical guitar which I had for a year or so, and then it was stolen. It's given me facility for building my own instruments. But during the Spoonful I never had really the time to do it.

I am now in the process of rebuilding a guitar. It's an instrument that I've always wanted to play, but I've just never had the time to take a little piece of broken glass and scrape the lacquer off and just fine down some of the insides and improve on what factories release as guitars. Very often you can take what little you know from a classical instrument and make a better sound out of a steel instrument.

I don't remember not playing the harmonica. It happened so fast. There were harmonicas lying around, and it's such an easy children's instrument.

What put me on to the Autoharp was falling madly in love with a lady when I was sixteen years old who owned one. And I figured the only way I could make it with her was to play a little guitar and learn how to play her Autoharp. She lent me her Autoharp and I kept it all winter and learned how to play it.

John Sebastian

From anyone else John Sebastian's approach would be mawkish. From Sebastian, though, the warmth is so real that you believe! His songs are children's songs—the past as recollected by an adult. They're like someone looking back into the innocence of youth, the magic of being a child—as he sees it.

He is the biggest optimist in pop music today. For example, in "Rainbows All Over Your Blues." It's a wistfulness. All delicate and muted emotions. Always a hint of nostalgia, which he shares with McCartney.

Audience

Sebastian is a groove. A phenomenal harmonica player. He and Charlie McCoy are still my favorite harmonica players.

Felix Pappalardi/Mountain

John Sebastian is like one of the absolute best, one of the most positive cats we got. And one of the most beautiful, most creative, and most highly evolved. He's one of the finest men on the planet. Absolutely one of the finest cats that's runnin' anywhere near me that I can see.

He does tie-dye that will make your brain fall right out . . . can't believe it.

David Crosby/Crosby, Stills, Nash and Young

Donovan

Donovan

Donovan is a saint.

Audience

I heard him call himself a folk singer. It's like looking at something from so many different angles. I have been struck on several occasions with his poetry, but by the same token I have been moved by his lyrics on several occasions. The first time I heard him, I said, "My God! A folk singer from England who plays just like Jack Elliott. I can't believe it!" I mean because there wasn't even anybody in this country that could play clean as Jack Elliott. Matter of fact, that was what Bobby said about him the first time he heard him play. Yeah. 'Cause I said that about him and then later I saw *Don't Look Back* and in *Don't Look Back* Don came to play for Dylan and that was what Dylan said. He leaned toward somebody and said something about Jack Elliott. We both had the same flash about Don. Which is not to say that Don's guitar style is by any means limited to that style, but it's mainly a compliment as to the clarity with which he picks. He also plays the same kind of guitar as I like—big fat Gibsons, 'specially J-45s.

I remember when he had first written "Happiness Runs" when I was over there. I went up to his cottage with David, Graham, and Stephen. We sat there all night long picking and singing, and he taught us that, and we did a round on it, you know, "Happiness runs in a circular motion, happiness runs . . ." and it, oh boy!!

John Sebastian

JAZZ ROCK

The Flock

We're not trying to restrict ourselves. We're just really trying to flow with whatever is happening. We just have so many ideas, we can't confine ourselves to certain boundaries. We don't want to prostitute ourselves to one category because it's not really us. We used to be a big soul band in the Midwest before Jerry (Goodman) was in the group. . . . He was way out. It was a little strange to get into this new thing.

Jerry Smith

I'm always experimenting with sounds. There's so many unused possibilities with amplifiers. If I find a new thing, I kind of play with it. If I found a certain note on that particular instrument—I think it's like a very high G or G-sharp—it comes out when I vibrate it really heavily. The sound doesn't stay outside of your ears, but it comes inside and starts pushing your eardrums—in and out. I found it's not really a sound that you hear, but it's a sound that you feel. So I play drums on the violin now with my fingers, and this is just another thing. People react very strangely to it. Like I find it funny sometimes that I actually get applause for hitting a note that's blowing their ears off. I don't have to generally, but that's a weapon. I use it as an outlet sometimes. If something's happening I don't dig, I hold the note for five minutes.

Jerry Goodman

We're not a superamplification group. We do some loud things, but that's not our thing. We have a lot of very dynamic changes—come down very low.

The Flock

The problem with having a lot of people together is that everyone has to really stay mellow through whatever crisis rises. I think we have been doing a fairly good job of it. Any kind, any kind. Not usually musical. They can't be. We straighten those out.

We come on stage with the same feeling about our physical appearances as we do about our music, which is like whatever we are. That's what we are on stage. What we have we are doing musically. Whatever we feel we should be doing musically, we do that.

Jerry Goodman and Jerry Smith

Jethro Tull

Jethro Tull is fantastic! It's just something about it, the sound of everything. They're fantastic live, but the flute and drum thing . . . their music is not definable. It's the most emotional of all the English music. Ian Anderson gets up there and has some kind of rapport with the audience. It's just emotion.

Audience

Nina Simone

She's dynamite. Anybody who'd follow her would be crazy. I wouldn't follow Nina Simone!

Roger McGuinn/The Byrds

One of my biggest problems, all my life I fight always to keep an equilibrium about music in that I'm one of those persons—I didn't have electronic instruments, but I was so gifted that I used to couldn't sleep and at times now I can't. Tunes—you can get it all in your head where you can't turn it off. You hear me? Where you can not turn it off! It is a thing. All of life is in that. And you have to know about it. You have to know things about it.

That's me. I never had any choice about it. There's a whole love/hate relationship that I have with my music. At times I talk to it and talk to the piano and things. Because it's another thing. There is such a thing as things being too good. And there are times when music can be like that. I wouldn't give it up. I can't. But it's just not what they think it is. That's not all it is.

Nina Simone

Nina Simone

The Liverpool Scene

We're not a group. We're five individuals.

Two or three summers ago, when there was a real kind of employment thing for musicians and all the groups weren't working, we decided we'd try to make a kind of permanent thing out of poetry and music.

I met this guitarist, Andy Roberts, who was working as a kind of solo folk musician. He worked with Roger McGough and me doing a whole lot of music to our poetry—just on acoustic guitar. This became quite a popular thing, and we got lots of demands to go to places. And so what eventually happened was that we went and I would get letters saying would you come and read poems, or would you and Andy Roberts come and do a poems-and-music thing. And I'd write back and say, "Why don't you have the group?" You know, in costume. We find it more interesting. Originally our work was all to do with colleges and universities and hospitals and things like that.

This year through to summer we've got a complete change in where we work. We now work mostly in blues clubs and places. It's a terrific kind of change of audience. We do universities and things, still, but we don't do it half as much—unless it's done out of purely a music thing. And this is really, I think, marvelous. We're moving from a rather specialist art sort of thing into a much more kind of open sort of more popular thing. The reason I think we always go very well with audiences is because we were always very conscious of programming. You don't do two things the same, one after each other. That's an elementary kind of mistake that nobody in straight sort of entertainment makes. You never do two slow sentimental songs one right after another. Poets doing poetry readings tend to do that, tend to read all the same things. And we were always very conscious of having the right kind of thing to start with and a good one to finish on and what to put in the middle and how to vary it and things.

We do a very noisy kind of abandoned thing. We always tend to do it as a choir. We do a funny one and a serious one—things like that. So that we're not hitting people over the head with things.

People change instruments a lot and things like that. We tend to only play together, as a band with a lead vocal, only about the last twenty minutes each night, which is a kind of rave, up thing that we do at the end of the night.

Adrian Henri

Jerry Goodman

FUSION: FOLK PLUS JAZZ EQUALS ROCK

Quicksilver Messenger Service

The name Quicksilver came about because we're all the same astrological sign: Virgo. Gary and Greg are born on the same day. David and I are born on the same day. The four of us were doing our thing. There was a fifth member then, Jimmy Murray, who is a Gemini. Virgos are mercury and mercury is quicksilver and Mercury is a messenger and Virgo is a servant, so Quicksilver Messenger Service. The name is expanded, and it still makes sense. It's still the same.

John Cipollina

We all like good old rock and roll. That's what gets us all together. We're all like of really varied musical backgrounds. Like how we started. I started playing the violin when I was five. And John (Cipollina), his mother was a pianist and she taught him how . . . classical piano for twelve years, forced him to, so of course he won't touch the piano now. And Nicky was educated classically, but on the side, I think, probably when he was supposed to be practicing, he was really playing Fats Domino stuff, you know.

Rock is the only thing you can say about it. Just a rock and roll band. That's the definition. The instruments make it a rock and roll band.

David Freiberg

I was always with Quicksilver. We just found out about it just recently, that's all. That's how it was, pretty much.

Dino Valente

It's a thing that gradually happened. I came over to do two or three week sessions with Steve Miller's album. David and John came up to see me while I was working on that, and they said that they were going to be doing an album pretty soon, and could I stay on, you know, and play on it, which was fine by me because I really didn't want to go home at that time and I should have done some things. So I was really glad of an excuse to stay for a few more weeks. I don't know, I just got into it, into their music, and into where I was at as well.

It was gradual, as well; it was just a thing where I was gettin' more and more into the band and their music and I really began diggin' that. . . .

Nicky Hopkins

A lot of people in Frisco, they're sitting down a lot more at dances. They want to hear the music. They want a little more out of it now than just the rhythm, so a lot of people are getting into timbres and tonalities and into lyrics, the lyrical tonalities, but I think that some of 'em are still a little too soft. I'd like to really be able to be pretty and still be kickin' all the time. That's what I think this band can do.

Dino Valente

John Cipollina

The Youngbloods

Being in a band means a lot of things. It means knowing how to play your instrument in the context of the musical group you're in. Learning to live together, learning to travel together, learning to be under pressure together, learning to be insulted together, learning to be loved together, and learning to get along really good. The better you get along as people, the better you play. Although you leave a certain part of you behind, you really got to get inside one another.

Money doesn't glorify us anymore. The thing we've gotten into playing together is more valuable. What we've learned is so valuable and so rare. I just never thought we would ever get this far together as we have. It really surprised me. It surprised all of us. Blew our minds. We'd almost given up. Wow, it's really good.

We had a reputation a long time ago when we first started out, and we got it from being very particular, working very hard and putting our things together with a great deal of care. Then we changed over to a trio and launched into a whole other thing of looking for freedom and improvisation. We found that we had played together long enough and learned enough about each other so we could actually improvise well enough together, follow each other, and feel each other so that it sounded as good, if not better than, the things we had created in a much more premeditated way. There is a state that you get into when you play your best. It's like locking into each other, emotionally, with your mind and everybody's physical things, everybody's technique, everybody's muscles working right, and then the ideas starting to move. One idea will pop up from me or Joe or Banana, and everybody starts to follow it and it moves like that and it is. I don't know how to explain it, it is just a state that I guess all musicians get into when they are tuned in enough to each other to be completely free. I guess this is what jazz has always been all about. Some people say, "Hey, a lot of your new stuff is like jazz," and I guess that's what they mean. It is a higher state to have reached, not the jazz, but being able to get into that; it's a phenomenon every time it happens, like I don't know what, a séance. But there's nothing stoned about it in a heavy sense, in a fumbly sense, but just like clear mountain stream water. You can see everything.

Jesse Colin Young

The Youngbloods

MOTOWN

Fantastic the way Motown makes a record. I don't think anybody makes a record like them. They make them the way Ford makes cars. It goes on an assembly line. Everybody gets a chance at producing it. They don't have like one producer. Whoever does the best job—whoever does the best mix on it —they pick out the best and it's like a tremendous corporation. They have some writers up there! They are really fantastic: Brian Holland and those people!

Felix Cavaliere/The Rascals

We dig the music, we dig the Temps and the Four Tops. Motown has so much formula stuff that only once in a while one of their real compositions will come out, and those are the ones—"Grapevine." That right there is justification for the whole other thing because "Grapevine" is so down, man, it's unbearable. Can't dig the formula stuff, but you know when they're doin' somethin' for real, and that's when you can dig it.

MC 5

I would say that Motown is the only sound I've really heard that I could say, well, you turn it on and, yeah, that came out of Motown.

I think part of the success of the Motown sound was the sound of Holland-Dozier-Holland, the sound of Smokey Robinson, the sound of Berry Gordy, the

sound of Fuqua and the guys that write with him. You can listen to a thing that Gordy produced and you listen to a thing produced by Harvey Fuqua. And they'll sound entirely different. Because Harvey is basically a very funky, bluesy kind of guy, whereas Holland and Dozier had a tendency to be more up- town. More uptown than that. The Fantastic Four, if you please. Whenever people talk about the Fan- tastic Four, they talk about the Motown sound. And the Fantastic Four to me were nothin' like Motown. They were more in a Curtis Mayfield bag than they were in a Motown bag.

Jerry Butler

They got such a great system, though. They got writers, arrangers, musicians, sidemen, singers, and it really works. The trouble with white people— they're all doin' it themselves, which is a groovy trip, but it doesn't always work.

Marty Balin/Jefferson Airplane

Motown kind of made Detroit a little more than a motor city. Before that that's all we had was cars.

Martha Reeves

Martha Reeves and the Vandellas

She's the greatest lady performer in the world! I just dig everything about her. She's just so dyna- mite. At the Apollo Theater, one amateur night, she came and sat in our box, and I've been madly in love with her ever since. She's just the classiest lady of all time.

Danny Fields

I sang in high school. I was featured soloist in my graduation class. I sang first soprano in a couple of concerts. One of the things I did that I really liked was the "Hallelujah." It was my first experience with an audience. After that, I got out of school and I decided that I'd like to sing. I started singing in nightclubs. I was underage, but nobody could tell. After that, I started rehearsing with some girls to sing and we had a group, you know. I wound up with a job at Motown as secretary, and one day I just brought the girls in, and from there it's been like wow.

Martha Reeves

Martha Reeves

Stevie Wonder

I've always been very religious. I do believe there's a God, a supreme being, 'cause how else can it be? How else can we have the ability to feel if there was not, or how else could we have the ability to feel, to express, to have emotional feelings about things?

I use to belong to a holiness church, and they heard me singing that rock and roll music and they told me I had to go. I wasn't suppose to sing rock and roll, but I was a bad little boy.

I was auditioned by Ronnie White who sings background with the Miracles. The talent scout at that particular time was Brian Holland. He auditioned me and told me I would have to come to the studio the next day for an audition with Berry Gordy. Mr. Gordy auditioned me, and they didn't sign me right away, but eventually, at the age of ten, he finally signed me and so we started.

We worked for about three years and eventually we came up with "Fingertips," which was my first record to be very popular. It was number one and I had a number-one album. I think I was the first artist to have number-one record and number-one album at the same time.

Stevie Wonder

When he gets onstage, he doesn't want to stop. He loves it. That's a beautiful thing, this business could do that for a blind boy.

Felix Cavaliere/The Rascals

I remember someone gave me a harmonica to put on my key chain, a little, small four-hole harmonica, and I started playing the blues, Jimmy Reed's blues, Bobby Blue Bland's. I use to sit by my radio and listen. Took a little of everybody's style and made up my own.

I think a harmonica for a long time was not really considered an instrument, and it is an instrument. As a matter of fact, I would consider—it's like a really small sax or something. There's so much you can do with it. I try to play it with a sax feeling. I'm crazy about the harmonica. You can express the way you feel. It's another color of music. You can get a vocal quality. Depends on how you play. If you put yourself into it like I put myself into it and try to express the way I would sing a song, then I only play the harmonica. You see, for instance, if I were singing a song, I would do it with the same basic; same anticipation, etcetera.

Stevie Wonder

Smokey Robinson and the Miracles

Smokey's one of the few people who make me cry when they perform—his voice is so sweet—like when he does "Ooooo, Baby, Baby."

Audience

Ah, yes, Smokey. . . .

Joe Cocker

He's one of the giant heavies of all time in rock and roll. Oh, I'd say, among other things, he's definitely influenced me. Oh, yes, definitely. Both as a singer and a songwriter, he is absolutely, you know, one of those real singular people, you know, he's one of the people that you can't, you can't approximate Smokey Robinson, you can only listen to him.

He's not what you call a screamer. But on the other hand, I mean, like for the same shot I used to go to the Apollo, there were people that would blow their sweet chops out for their half hour onstage, but Smokey would come out and do that, and odd, you know, like I mean I'll never forget like this three-hundred-pound chick that stood up and just swooned when he started to sing. She was right next to me and she really, she came right in on me. A huge black chick in a fantastic white polka-dotted dress that made her look just even bigger and a funny hat on, you know, was the whole shot, and she collapsed right on me, and that said it for me!

John Sebastian

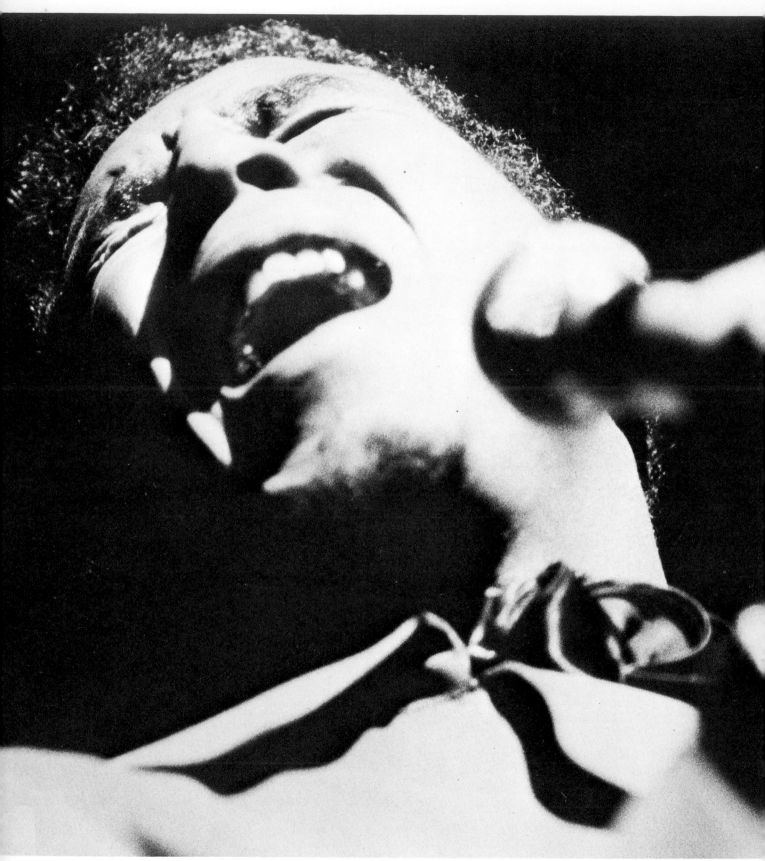

Smokey Robinson

Gladys Knight and the Pips

Gladys Knight and the Pips—they're *bad!* They're movin' in a straight—whew! "Nitty Gritty"—favorite song of all time. Sure is.

MC 5

We all started in church. Most of what I believe they call rhythm and blues singers today started in church. And really, I believe this is where the soul sound came from. It's the delivery, the way it's done, the way the person is singing a song.

I don't want to be typed. I don't want people to say, "Gladys Knight and the Pips—that's a rock and roll group." I don't want that. I want them to say that we are entertainers. I mean if you dig country and western music, we can do a little country and western for you. If you dig a little soft-shoe, if you dig getting down to the nitty-gritty, if you dig the slow ballads, I want them to know that Gladys Knight and the Pips is the group we can get to do it. I don't want to be classed as a rock and roll group.

Gladys Knight

Gladys Knight and the Pips

David Ruffin

My mother died when I was eleven months old. My father passed in '57. And most of my life, I've been on my own, tryin' to do my thing. Everybody has to go out and face the reality of life. That's what everybody's got to do. Do your own thing. Strength is your own thing, you know.

David Ruffin

The first time I heard his voice I couldn't believe somebody could sing that way. Every successive record he ever had I just bought it. And then, oh, boy, when he left the group, I sure checked the group off my list fast.

He was it. There's no a . . . there's never been—for my money—a lead singer with that group, I mean, regardless of his time that he's done now separate from it, from the group. I remember going to the Apollo, like I knew about David Ruffin probably before you did just because I was conscious of like peculiar musicians that I really dug, you know. And the first couple of tunes that I heard, I said, "Good God, man. How can he get through a tune singing that way?" I used to go and see him and the thing that always killed me was the way that . . . I mean like there were the Temptations and they were outa sight and they sure did their routines great. But the stuff that Ruffin used to get into just standing there. I remember like he used to come out with the sunglasses on and like all the Blood in the audience was freaking out right before he even started singing 'cause he looked so cool. There's nobody that ever looked as cool as David Ruffin. His wrists are at least six inches long. He'd stand out there and do his thing. I remember he'd come out and he'd snap his cuffs and he does a thing with his tie . . . and all his songs, he really used to act out all those songs. Did you ever see him do "I Wish It Would Rain"? He does all this stuff. But it's like, I mean, it's really hard to pull off that kind of stuff without really looking like an idiot. And David Ruffin—he looked like a prince doin' it.

John Sebastian

David was with the Dixie Nightingales. David was about fourteen, and he was a little skinny guy, real skinny, and he was singin' gospel songs. He sang with so much feeling, just listening to him, he'd go all through you. You'd just have to sit there and hold yourself to keep from shoutin'. Cleotha couldn't keep herself from shoutin'. She just had to let herself go. But I'd fight it. You see, he was *bad!*

Daddy thought that the Dixie Nightingales were such a good group he booked them on some of our things with us. The next thing we heard he was with the Temptations. He still kept the same thing. You can tell from the songs that he sings, it's still, by him singin' gospel like that. And changin' to what he was doin' with the Temptations didn't necessarily have to take anything from him as far as his feelings for God was concerned, you see, 'cause it's in him. You get it as a child. It's just in you. It's just like your parents raise you right. You grow up with that and you don't stray. So like what David had in him, he still has it. And like a lot of people say, like that boy left church and he's singin' the blues now, and he's goin' to the devil, but it's not like that. He can still be a Christian person and sing. It's a job. It's just the words are changed. And all of it is music. It's the same music. The words are changed. In fact, you can get closer to God when you change like that, because people talk, church people, the older people in the church talk in this vein, like he's goin' to the devil 'cause he's singin' pop songs. But what I hear in David's songs, in these love songs that he's singin', is the same thing I heard in his singin' those church songs. 'Cause I can feel them just like I could feel the gospel songs. All of it is a message. The songs he's singin' now is like to the lovers, people who are in love and they're not gettin' along, and like "World of Darkness": "I'm in a world of darkness/can't see no light/ no satisfaction/nowhere in sight" . . . so here he is, sittin' here, he evidently, he and his girl aren't makin' it, so he's singin' about it. He's just puttin' his thing into song. That's all there is to it. You can tell it's there, when he's singin' "Sunshine, blue sky/ Please. . . ." When he say "Please!" he's beggin'. You dig? Like he's just really honestly beggin', "Please go away!"

He has something that a lot of people don't have. It's something that you can't take away from him. I don't care what direction he goes in—if he's by himself or in a group or what—he's got that feelin' and you just can't take it away and everybody doesn't have it.

Mavis and Cleotha Staples/The Staple Singers

David Ruffin

BLUES

The blues express, I think, frustration, express a feeling of blues, of sadness, not saying that all the young white rock singers are sad, but I think that a lot of people in general are concerned about the situation that exists in the world today. The problems that we do have, I think even more than ever, it's like a cycle. It's like there was a time when people felt it and then they didn't feel it and then they felt it even stronger; then they didn't feel it and then even stronger. So blues have had a great influence. It used to be just a black singer would sing the blues. I got the blues. A lot of people got the blues today. It's beautiful 'cause we can relate with each other, can all relate to situations or relate very directly with that style of music. Like everybody can sing the blues or like when a funky tune is on, a lot of people can relate today. It's even more universal than a lot of other music.

Stevie Wonder

It always strikes me as a little bit incongruous to have guys coming over from England, leaping up on a stage, and singing about "dem old cotton-picking days down South."

Moody Blues

I like blues. I like blues played by people who got the blues. I mean, nobody can tell me that some skinny English guy's got the blues. Man, I mean you can't tell me that! I will refuse to believe that. I mean somebody who's got the blues is like John Lee Hooker. That gentleman is the living embodiment of everything you're talking about. In the flesh. He stands there before you naked as shit. Man, it's just unbearable. You're blown back by the sheer charge of the gentleman.

MC 5

B. B. King

B. B. King is an original guitar player. I've seen a hundred, maybe two hundred guitar players take that man's guitar style and make a fortune copyin' him. But this guy is the originator and he's still the greater, 'cause he was the first. But people put all kinds of psychedelical sounds over what he has did, and it makes their stuff sound different, so people hear their stuff and don't recognize that what a guy's playin' on a guitar ain't no different than what this man's been playin' for twenty-five years.

Dr. John, the Night Tripper

I'm not always talkin' about a woman. For instance, maybe I sing, "Baby this or baby that," I'm not always talkin' to a woman. It is a form of relief and people still whistle, and people still hum tunes. Happy or sad, they still hum. A lot of times this is just a way of gettin' the message over.

Everybody don't riot. You only has a few that do. Some people don't belive in riotin'. They believe in gettin' their points across. A lot of people don't believe in doin' some of the things that some people are doin'. Maybe this is the way it's supposed to be done, but a lot of us don't believe that. A lot of us believe that a lot of things that happened, we get hurt most in the end from doin' that. And I don't think that this, all the times, is the only way to focus the attention on the country—by bein' killed.

I think all black people can sing blues if they want to. I think they're not singin' them simply because they don't want to. I've had black people to tell me, "I've never listened to the blues. I've never liked them." I think that's an exaggeration. I believe that deep down in, every black person—and a lot of whites—has got blues.

In 1943 I went into the army and that's when I started to sing the blues. I found out that people paid more and better for blues than they did for spirituals. Many times we were singin' in church and they passed the hat around, and although people would sit there and enjoy your singin' they wouldn't put anything in the hat! But if you sing blues, you could charge admission.

Everybody's been tryin' to get ready for the social change in a way of speakin'. Like guys wearin' processed hair. A lot of this is due to wantin' to be accepted. For a long time the black people felt that

B. B. King

unless you dressed a certain way, looked a certain way, you wasn't really accepted. And just recently the people began to be proud that they are black and feel like they do have dignity. It's just like people that have had amnesia for a long time and just now beginnin' to come back to themselves. So, there's nothin' bad about bein' yourself. Why be ashamed of it? So you're black. You're a blues singer. Yes, you're a blues singer. Well, people sing blues. Why be ashamed of it? I think the kids today, a lot of 'em don't like it 'cause kids love to dance. So as far as the blues singer, or the slow blues singer like myself, it isn't that they actually hate it; they don't really like it because it isn't something to dance off of, but they're beginnin' to say, "Yes, that's my man. That's B. B." or whoever it might be.

B. B. King

B. B. King

Johnny Winter

I was about four or five, maybe six, I started playing clarinet, and I was really into clarinet. I was probably going to be another Artie Shaw or Benny Goodman, except I had to have braces. They told me I would have a really bad overbite if I didn't quit playing clarinet. Wrecked my whole life. I was really unhappy about it.

So I drowned my sorrows in a ukulele after a while because daddy played ukulele and I decided, well, that's cool, and it's nice 'cause I could sing, too. Then my hands got bigger, so I decided the guitar would be cool. It really would have been strange if I had continued playing clarinet. At the time, when I was five, it seemed like the right thing to do. It was really exciting to play clarinet.

No particular person wiped me out. It was just the whole idea of blues music turned me on to the whole thing at once. I had never heard any blues and then all of a sudden I wanted to hear just about everybody that played it. It excited me because it was something different. I could name people that I picked up things from. Millions of them, like Otis Rush, Magic Sam, Lightnin' Slim, Slim Harpo and Lightnin' Hopkins, Muddy Waters, Son House. Just everybody, but it wasn't only blues you know. Blues was what I liked personally, but there were others, all the people on the Top 40 stations—Carl Perkins, Little Richard, Fats Domino, Elvis Presley—and just music. You just pick up, you just assimilate from everywhere. But blues was what I happened to like personally. Because it seemed like more personal music.

Most music seemed to be created for the music itself, whereas blues seemed like a personal communication thing, a spur-of-the-moment flow of consciousness type thing, improvisation more than any-

Johnny Winter

thing else. You just got up there. Whatever you felt like, it came out at the particular time. A different way each time you did the same song. There wasn't as much to tie you down as a real wide, just three-chord pattern. There wasn't a particular melody line. You could just make up anything. It's real un-inhibiting. It's real free.

Most people can't get into straight blues with no trimmings. They need the repetition of the stan-dardized melody lines to have something to hold onto. You have to be pretty involved in it to really enjoy it. I think the musicians in most cases feel the music more than the average person—certainly the average teeny-bopper that turns on the radio. So the thing to do is try to dress it up, not to degrade it, but put enough into it that you have to to attract people to it and they say enough of what you want to say and feel like it's real and groovy. Put it together to make it reach as many people as you can, 'cause if people don't dig it at all, you've lost them completely. There's nobody there. You've got to do both. You've got to play the music and try to reach people, too. So I think there is a trend to get away from doing just blues. Blues can be boring to a musician, too. It's fun to be uninhibited and just be able to play everything you want to, but it's also fun to create things and create musical forms which with blues you really don't do. It's just a flowing out of what you have to say. There's no structure there. You don't have to confine yourself. You don't have to really think things out. You just try to do a little bit of everything.

Johnny Winter

Elvin Bishop

Now you take my position what I was in when I was in high school in Tulsa, Oklahoma. I went to this high school, called Will Rogers High School. That's the kind of people they name high schools after there. I sort of didn't exactly fit in, you know, I mean I was makin' it because I was real smart and everything, you know. I screwed around a lot in school, but I always made it by. And when I got this scholarship, there was just nothing they could say. They had been threatening me with not being able to get into college all the time, and I got that. But I couldn't understand exactly why I didn't fit in. I was there and I had never been exposed to anything unusual outside of this mainstream of America shit. Except this blues on the radio, and that was like something real strong, and it just identified with the intense feeling of you. I knew something was missing in my life. I just went straight for it and dived into it headlong. It took me about five or six years to realize that it wasn't just the blues that I really dug. The blues wasn't all that was good in life or in musical forms. It took me a long time to stop trying to identify with colored people exclusively, and I started digging jazz, Indian music, country and west-ern, and everything else. Actually, when I finally get down to my own final me music, it's going to be a mixture of all of these things, and it won't be straight blues.

It's real easy to, if you dig the feeling of something, like I was saying about blues, to go ahead and try to swallow it whole. Adopt all the trappings as well as the things that you dig about it. It's kind of hard. It takes a certain amount of maturity to pick out the pieces that you really dig from it and leave the rest alone 'cause it doesn't fit you. I went through that thing of wearing Continental suits and Italian shoes and shit, and using Dixie Peach on my hair and stuff like that.

Elvin Bishop

Elvin Bishop

John Mayall

John Mayall

There's certain blues bands that I respect. Like John Mayall. I think he believes in what he's doing. It's so easy to leap on a stage and play a load of twelve bars; it's easy to con people by doing that. And I think a lot of bands have done that. I mean, there's very few really—really into it blues bands. I think John Mayall is about the only really English blues bloke.

Ray Thomas/Moody Blues

The Elvis thing was part of the big pop business. They were the chart toppers. There was only a small handful of blues followers. But there's been that same interest in the whole of Europe—in blues and American music in general—that would never happen in the country of its origin. I mean that could never happen. Something that a country has, that's taken for granted, but to somebody in a foreign country, if it's an art form, it doubles in its importance because it's not available to them, so a great deal of study, interest, and research goes into it. As I say, there's always been an interest in jazz and blues. By comparison with Americans' interest, it has been phenomenal since the twenties. . . .

John Mayall

Taj Mahal

Taj Mahal, he's one of those cats that you can't put in a bag very easily, because he's well into his own thing. He's going to be a lot more into it soon. He used to do exclusively country blues for a living. He tried . . . I remember, he had this group called the Seven Sons or the Sons of something in L.A. But anyway, what he was doing then was taking country blues in a chunk and putting it into an electric band setting. But he's way beyond that now. He has like white country influences, and he has R & B influences, and he has electric blues influences, and he has country blues influences, and he's melted them down very nicely into his own personal thing, I think.

His guitar player, Jesse Owen Davis, is from Oklahoma. He's had a lot of background in country music and you can hear it in his playing. He played with guys like Conway Twitty.

Elvin Bishop

I believe that blues are bigger now than they ever have been. Because now a lot of white kids are beginnin' to like blues, and black kids are beginnin' to realize that this is a part of us.

B. B. King

B. B. King

FUSION: BLUES/ROCK

Ten Years After

I think blues will travel a considerable way and the blues-based thing will develop a lot more before anything entirely new emerges.

First, I'd say the object of so-called white blues or English blues isn't to recreate that, personalize it as a similar thing. To a degree, when we sing a bluesish song we are relating to the way it was sung, but more in the style than in the folklore. The second point is a good actor could give over the same feeling as your black blues singers who've been through the "cotton fields." There again, a lot of the black blues singers are acting as well. Usually find that the black singers from the "cotton fields" don't make it. Usually the amount of theatrics thrown in. . . .

The music we're creating is closely related to blues basically. It's like a basic carrier format. There are a lot of other things as well—influences. You know, jazz, blues, rock, swing. . . .

I personally don't relate to American blues. Groups stem from American blues, as did the Beatles stem from American R & B and solid rock sort of thing, but it finds its own character after a while. I'd like to think we're heading toward our own character.

A lot of different events and circumstances and influences over a considerable time brought me to where I am now. Originally, my family said I should play an instrument. I played the clarinet, which didn't really work. The clarinet led me to the guitar. I listened to Benny Goodman on clarinet. He had a very good guitarist, Charlie Christian. I listened to Charlie Christian and started guitar lessons and then got wrapped up in the rock thing when that came out. I got into blues and such from discovering rock and its basics.

I wasn't saying I was going to be a jazz musician. I was just interested in music and I was leaving it all to chance. I wasn't thinking of it particularly as a profession. Jazz seems somewhat more commanding to me as a musician, because it is something you can get into technically.

I want a lot more control over things which I'm not capable of doing yet. I don't like wow-wow. I think that it's just a gimmick which has its place. We've used wow-wow on albums to get an effect over, but there's no individual characteristics of a guitarist on a wow-wow pedal. It sounds like anyone using a wow-wow. You can only really use it in one way. It's such an individual sound that it's difficult—it's impossible to do anything new with it. I'm into developing things like that, but as yet, you know, I'm still prodding and experimenting.

Alvin Lee

The Doors

The Doors are basically a blues-oriented group with heavy dosages of rock and roll, a moderate sprinkling of jazz, a minute quantity of classical influence, and some popular elements. But basically, a white blues band.

Our music has returned to the earlier form, just using the four instruments. We felt that we had come too far in the other direction, i.e., orchestration, and wanted to get back to the basic format.

Jim Morrison

Alvin Lee

Led Zeppelin

Led Zeppelin is a good name, isn't it? I made it up. Everybody says Keith Moon made it up, but he didn't. About four tours ago I was really gettin' fed up with The Who. I was fed up with gettin' no recognition for my writing or my bass playing, and I was really getting depressed. And I was talking with a fellow who is the production manager for the Led Zeppelin now. I was talking to him down in a club in New York. And I said, "Yeah, I'm thinking of leaving the group and forming my own group. I'm going to call the group Led Zeppelin. And I'm going to have an LP cover with like the *Hindenburg* going down in flames, and, you know, this whole business." And like two months later he was working for Jimmy Page and, like, they were looking for a name, and so he suggested Led Zeppelin, and Page liked it, and they came out with the same LP cover that I'd planned. I don't know whether the group knows that I made it up. I think they think that Keith made it up because Keith was there, and like Jimmy Page came up to Keith and said, "Thanks for the name." And Keith said, "All right," you know, sort of takin' the credit. I just have to think up a new name for my new group. I'm good at group names . . . surprise myself.

John Entwistle/The Who

If Robert Plant had been a contemporary of Charles Darwin, *The Origin of Species* would have been scrapped, along with the whole theory about evolution from the apes. One look at Plant in action is living proof of the infusion of the divine into the race of man!

Audience

Mountain

My basic education was in classical music. My first instrument was piano. My second was viola. I play a little guitar. I didn't actually start playing bass, which I'm playing now, until I actually started playing with Tim Hardin in the Village, where I started playing electric bass with him. And trumpet at the University of Michigan, where I went to study conducting and music literature. So these other things —like going down to the Village after I got out of the army and being exposed to folk music, becoming close friends with Mississippi John Hurt and playing with him, and playing with people like Tom Paxton, Joan Baez, so many people in the folk field —widened an already pretty broad musical education. I don't feel I've arrived at any complete thought yet. I'm still looking. And Mountain is a reflection of that thought process.

I met Leslie (West) about a month after I had completed "Disraeli Gears" with Cream. I was frankly knocked out with Leslie's approach to his guitar and equally knocked out by his approach to me, which was, I would say, unlike most of the people I've met: not very loud and very, what I consider, sane. Leslie does have respect for me, but that's not the whole thing. The thing is I can be with Leslie over an extended period of time and not want to beat him up. I like him. He's my friend.

We plan to evolve a tremendous amount from where we are now. Leslie's a terrific acoustic guitar player, and we did a lot of things on his album with acoustic instruments.

The function of the organ in our band is not what Booker T.'s is in Booker T. and the MG's. He plays texture. You're not totally all the time aware of the fact that he's doing that, but if the organ stopped, you'd miss it. It's very subtle. It's not the kind of thing that sticks out. But like in rehearsal a lot of times he'll stop, and it's just a hole that you could drive a truck through.

We're going to work on a couple of things where we sing together. It's one of the things that I think we have that's very unique. Leslie's got a very edgy voice and mine is silken.

I just hope we can please a lot of people.

Felix Pappalardi

Leslie West

Peter Green

Fleetwood Mac

Peter Green proved to the audience who thought there could only be one Eric Clapton that somebody else could play and he can be good, too. Then gradually Peter had to go through the whole scene of being compared with Eric, which was a hang-up, and with the passage of time he's proved to be totally different. He sounded a bit like Eric when he first joined, but it didn't take long before he was sounding like Peter.

John Mayall

Steppenwolf

Steppenwolf sings with feelin' and he stands up there and sing. He don't be doin' no clownin' and do. I respect a person that does that, that stand up and sing instead of runnin' around and jumpin' around. And he's sexy. He stands with his legs apart. He knows where he's goin'.

Mavis Staples/The Staple Singers

When I came into Canada, I managed to scrounge up some money and buy this beat-up guitar, which is like the typical schlock legend bullshit: Hank Williams-got his-cigarbox-guitar-at-the-age-of five and all this. I hacked around on that, doing country and western music between about fourteen and seventeen, finished high school, then went to the States. The folk revival was just happening. The country and western thing that I had been doing was sort of a semi part of that folk thing. I dug just about everything—Cajun music, hillbilly, bluegrass, Elizabethan ballads, and Appalachian things.

I got into this thing with the public library, the music library, getting these Library of Congress early field recordings all the way back to the days of the work song recorded live, almost live, at Sugarland Work Farm in Texas. So I started from scratch. My intention had been to go to UCLA after finishing high school to take folklore and folk music, graduate, play it, and teach it. I thought I was free from direction, having finished high school. It wasn't so. They stuck me with all these other things that I didn't want to take.

I was bummin' around for a couple of years in both countries, Canada and the States, with a guitar, a duffel bag, and a sleeping bag. Playing dives and bars and coffeehouses and joints. It was a great life in a way. It was a bit trying at times, standing in the heat on the highway for three or four hours, but by and large I always had enough bread to get from one place to the next. There were always a few groovy people to exchange music and ideas with and all this. When I arrived in Toronto, Canada, on one of my return visits, I was playing in Yorkville Village. Next door was playing this group, the Sparrow. I met one guy who was the pianist at a party. I was playing harmonica. It was this weird party with

John Kay

this country and western singer by the name of Johnny See and Lonnie Johnson, the old blues cat, and all sorts of weird people who just happened to be playing the Village at the time. We all jammed, these eight thousand acoustic guitars and five washtub basses and all these things. I was playing harmonica, and this pianist said, "Well, our bass player's trying to play harp because we're just slowly getting into a blues thing. Why don't you come by?" I went over there and I played a couple of numbers with them for fun during the rehearsal, and it turned out really good. So I went back a couple of nights between breaks in my set and sat in with them. I made up my mind that it would be a great idea to get more instruments to do the thing I was doing. And so, Goldie McJohn, who is our organist now, and I together joined the Sparrow to make it five people. We played Canada (that was in August)

until May of the following year (that was 1966). Then we came to New York and played Arthur, etcetera, for a length of time, had a manager, etcetera. We were on Columbia Records. They were always a year or two behind what was happening musically, so having played all these discotheques and stuff and not getting any further, we went to L.A. and did well at the Whiskey. The riots happened, and they closed down the Strip, and then we went to Frisco, and that's when we really got into some things. But Columbia still had this idiotic attitude. So not getting any support from the record company and not having any record success, we had like this stalemate. We disbanded and got a release from Columbia. Once I had that, I started the group Steppenwolf and did this whole thing with Dunhill.

On the first three albums there was a common quality of the instrumental. The music and the lyrical

content varied from the dance type things like "Sookie, Sookie" to "The Pusher" and "The Ostrich," which were more topical. It was a good thing we did it that way because we didn't want to get pegged as politics only. But as we went along, being interested in music and history and the combination of the two, I slowly got this idea that someday I was going to get into like a political-social concept album thing. I had actually intended to wait with it longer than last August, which is the time that we started on the *Monster* album.

John Kay

Steppenwolf, he's getting a message across. He's coming in there with that soulful thing. This is really something, because he's a white artist. I feel a chill go through me and when a chill goes through me I know that I dig this person.

Yvonne Staples/The Staple Singers

Steve Miller Band

Blues was the first thing I heard that I could imitate or learn from. And now after doing that for about ten years I feel I'm ready to start playing some of my own music. So do Lonnie and Tim. And that's what we're doing now. It's been described as hard rock. I guess maybe that's right to call it.

We used to call ourselves the Steve Miller Blues Band, and I was talking to Butterfield and Butterfield suggested that I don't do that because people always expect you to play nothing but classical blues everywhere you go, so I said okay.

Steve Miller

SOUL

Soul ain't nothin' but a feelin'. It gets in your hand—makes you clap your hand. Gets in your feet—makes you move your feet. That's all it is.

Wilson Pickett

Soul is communication. It's communication of the untouchable part of man. Soul is the thing that makes you cry when you hear a sad story or makes you laugh when you hear a funny story, because you can envision yourself physically into it, even though you've never physically experienced it. Soul is the ability to relate one's sorrow to somebody else's sorrow or one's happiness to somebody else's happiness, you know. It's like they use the term, "Well, man, that ain't my soul." You take like if a cat gets high, you know, he may get high on one thing and you might say, "Man, it doesn't move me at all." So like your soul doesn't really respond to his soul at that particular point. It goes back to one man's meat is another man's poison. The thing that feeds the spiritual me or the spiritual you is soul. That's a communication that's not touched or felt, but you know it's there. It's that anything that talks without saying anything. The fact that Ray Charles can say, "Georgia!" and Georgia becomes a woman, rather than a piece of earth or a state, and you can feel that he's really singing to a woman. That's what soul is all about. But we've made soul black, we've made soul food, we've made soul whatever. But basically it all means the same thing. It all means communication. Like when I say a person is a soul brother, to me that means he and I can communicate because we've suffered the same things and we don't have to talk about it. Because we can just look at each other and say, "Yeah, you've been there." When we talk about soul food, it's the communication that we know what we like. I imagine to Jewish people gefilte fish is soul food, because they know that that's where it's at as far as they're concerned.

Like I listen to Jimmy Smith play. And though I've never played, he plays exactly the way I would play. So when he makes the thing, I'll say, "Yeah!" because if I had made it at that moment, that's how I would have done it.

Like I knew he was going to do that before he did it. And the fact that he did it—that was the communication. It was like my mind moving his hands, you know.

And I think that this is the thing that happens with an audience or like when Aretha does "The Weight," and she does "yah-da-da-da-da-da," I say, "Yeah! Put the weight on me!" 'Cause I can feel that that's what she's gonna do. I know what's gonna happen. Curtis (Mayfield), you know, (sings), "Some people say we ain't got the right. . . . This is my country. . . ." It's such a great statement! It's so soft and, man, like anybody who's ever been through that kind of thing can just feel this song. And that's what it is. Like you sit there and you see a little black record spinnin' around, and the record is unimportant spinnin' around. It's what you're hearing and what it makes you feel. That is really fantastic!!

Jerry Butler

Soul musicians are playin' music to which you can dance. They always have been and they always will. Soul music is gettin' up and movin'. It's got your heart beatin' and your guts movin'. A soul record comes on the radio and it goes directly to your cells. That's what it's designed for. . . . It's got that incredible human quality to it that you have to dig.

MC 5

I knew that there was prejudice, you know, the outside world. But I never thought there was any in music. But I'm beginning to see now, I don't care how good you are, if you're a black artist you still got that one against you. You know, even if you're fantastic. And most of the good black artists are better than the good white artists, let's put it that way, at what they do. They're much more honest about it. That thing still exists 'cause Wilson Pickett could knock any of those people dead. Kids don't really see a difference, but radio station owners seem to.

John Fogerty/Creedence Clearwater Revival

Steve Miller

The young people was starvin' for a groove, a beat, something that they could really get goin' behind, and let their hair down, and sock-it-to-'em. And rhythm and blues fell right into that thing at the right time. Rhythm and blues been around so long, it hadn't been exposed until so many kids started diggin' it. They can dance by it and they can really feel what they want to do.

A lot of people ask me, "How long do you think rhythm and blues is gonna last?" I think rhythm and blues is gonna last forever. They got all kinds of names for music now: they got underground music, psychedelic; to me it's all good. Because I think, big as this world is, you can have as many kinds of music as you want. An' you ain't never 'sposed to knock another groove. My next tune I'll call "Psychedelic Wicked." That's right. You got to keep goin'. Ain't no use to sayin', "Hey, this is what's goin' to happen forever," because things'll change.

You know what I mean? An' I'll bet you money I can get out there and sing me one of them underground songs just as quick as anybody else! If they think they're gonna stop me they got another thought comin'. I'm goin' out there and sock me one of them things to 'em.

Wilson Pickett

When I started singing, rhythm and blues was a lot of noise. Nobody was really interested in it but young people and the people that knew it were associated and lived with it. But when you mentioned it, it was like a dirty word. Nobody wanted to be bothered. It was just a thing that was layin' out there like country and western music. It was the bread and butter of the industry because you had an audience that was going out there and buy a Jimmy Reed, whether it was a great piece of material or not.

Jerry Butler

Otis Redding

I don't think Otis was a blues singer. If there's any truth in so-called "soul" singing, that's what he was.

B. B. King

Otis Redding was the sky and the clouds and the sunshine. He really was.

Marty Balin /Jefferson Airplane

Otis Redding was a natural prince. When you were with him he communicated love and a tremendous faith in human possibility. A promise that great and happy events were coming. In some magic way his recordings have the same inspirational quality.

Jerry Wexler

My man Otis, every time he got up there you knew it. The cat would be stompin' holes in the floor. Volcanoes would be rising, he was stompin' so hard. He almost tore the stage up at Monterey. Me and Michael Bloomfield was sittin' there, and I almost fell over in the audience, 'cause I was goin' right with him.

Buddy Miles

I almost cry sometimes when I hear Otis's stuff. Stuff like that make you actually laugh—not laugh from "Oh, look at that, ha-ha-ha-ha!" But that real good feeling, and then you get lumps in your throat, and shit—yeah, that's when the stuff is poppin'. And if they keep on goin', I know I be embarrassed 'cause I know I'm goin' to cry. I say, "Oh, no, I got to get out of here!" But they be kickin'. That's American. That's American, that scene. Once that's respected, that's what's goin' to pull America out. The music, and the arts, blah-blah, woof-woof, you know.

Jimi Hendrix

The only persons who reached a certain peak in show business had to be killed. That was Sam Cooke, Frankie Lymon, Dinah Washington, and Otis Redding.

Martha Reeves

Since "Pain in My Heart," I was an Otis Redding fan. And I said, "Man, this cat is just so country and 'greasy,' you know, just so right to it." I said, "Oh, he's unbelievable!" The way he could say a word, and wasn't even a word, just "nhanhaaa!" I just knew that if anybody else had introduced "I've Been Lovin' You Too Long" to the world it would not have happened. That was his own slice of life. That was his thing. Fate just made it happen that way.

Jerry Butler

Aretha Franklin

Aretha was singin' "Never Grow Old" when I first heard her in Los Angeles, California, in person ('cause she had a record of "Never Grow Old"), but the first time I met Aretha was in Los Angeles in '55. We were out there with the Davis Sisters. It was a long time ago. We were young. Aretha was singing "Never Grow Old." She was playin' the piano. She and the little midget from the church, Sammy Bryant, were travelin' with Reverend Franklin. I knew Aretha's brother first. He said, "I want you to meet my sister Aretha." And we met Aretha and we got tight, and from then on, Aretha would come to Chicago, and Yvonne, Cleetie, and I would go to Detroit and take our vacation there, and she'd come to Chicago.

I thought she had a good voice, and I knew she could sing and play the piano, and a few runs that she made, I dug 'em, and I could feel 'em, but at that time I wasn't concentratin' on her enough, listenin' to her close enough, to really get into her, but I knew she had a lot goin' for her. She was just out there, 'cause her daddy had her out there.

Mavis Staples/The Staple Singers

Aretha is one of our greatest, and she's singing very hard. Not because she's a black woman or anything of the sort, but because she can sing. She can just natural born sing!

Sam & Dave

Wilson Pickett

I think Aretha is one of the greatest singers that we've ever had—and ever will have. Period.

B. B. King

It kind of scared me because Aretha said she's Eleanor Rigby, and Eleanor dies. She's like an instrument. Her voice is like a horn. The things she does with it frightens me to death . . . such freedom.

Martha Reeves

She wasn't a featured artist. Aretha was just an added attraction to her father. Her father was a great minister. He had several albums out. He was the featured artist. Sammy and Aretha were like added attractions and would sing one song each. Sammy would sing a song, and then Aretha would sing a song, and then her father would come out.

Cleotha Staples/The Staple Singers

She had all that she has now, she's just bringin' it out more now. She's pourin' it out more, but I don't think, she just didn't satisfy an audience. She wasn't tryin'. At the same time, he would only let her sing one song, which really wasn't enough time to get into what she was doin', and the song that she would sing was "Never Grow Old." Then the next thing I heard about was a couple of years later she made "Precious Lord" "live" in the church. At that time, we were kids. We were playful, and I wasn't payin' that much attention to . . . I knew she had it, like I listen to her now and listen to other singers now. I just wasn't listenin'.

Mavis Staples

You can't believe certain things, but you can believe Aretha!

Audience

The Impressions

Curtis has a sound. But I don't think that anybody else in Chicago has the sound that Curtis has. During the time that they were talking about the Chicago sound, well, Curtis was producing most of those things. That's basically what they were talking about was the "Curtis Mayfield sound."

Jerry Butler

We feel honestly, our first responsibility is to be good artists, good professional entertainers who can bring about good presentation and truly be entertaining to the audience. That's basically the first thing. We don't pretend nor are we trying to be political or anything else in reference to what we sing. We're only entertainers, and it just so happens that a lot of times I write songs about our times, and it should be because these are the trends. I shouldn't be writing back as to what was going on ten years ago, you know. They were hits, and I guess by fate or luck or whatever you want to call it. The public sort of adopted us as more or less something a bit more than artists or entertainers simply because of things we have said. We are not afraid to record anything if it's good music, and I'm happy to see that the public and our great fans recognize it as such, and they continue to support us.

Curtis Mayfield

I like the Impressions. I like that touch. I like that flavor, that type of music. It's like an enchanted thing if it's done properly. You see, everybody has their own ways of sayin' things, but the Impressions have been on the right track. They did a thing called "Keep on Pushin'." They did some really old songs back in there. They're some people that need to be really, really respected. See, these are classical composers. I don't care what their music sounds like today, because today, as things are happening at that particular time, the people that's in that particular time don't really know the value of it until it dies off. But now people really have to start learning the value of things as they're living today.

Jimi Hendrix

Yeah, yeah. Yeah, I like some of the things Curtis Mayfield's doing. He's like a Paul Kantner of soul. I dig him. That's how I put it together. He's like a Paul Kantner of soul. He's doin' the same thing—"If you had a choice of colors. . . ." You know, Paul's like that. He comes right up front and says things like that. Curtis has written some beautiful songs.

Marty Balin/Jefferson Airplane

Wilson Pickett

I guess I'm just about the most misunderstood singer in show business.

I got my share of friends in show business, and I got my share of people who think they hate me, and they don't, see, because they say, "Hey, I hate him. I don't like him!" And they sittin' right there on the front row. You understand me? Not one time. . . . two and three and four times. They keep comin' and they keep buyin' records. So if hatin' me make 'em do that, I'm a try an' think of some more things to make 'em hate me, 'cause, you know, that's really good!

Wilson Pickett

I like Pickett, some of his songs. I'll tell you two records that I really did buy: "Hey Jude" and "Hey Joe." I liked the beat he had on it, really, because I had heard it by the Beatles. I liked it also by the Beatles, but I tell you Pickett had more soul in there.

Yvonne Staples/The Staple Singers

I love Wilson Pickett!

Marty Balin/Jefferson Airplane

The Eskimos are buyin' rhythm and blues. You don't just depend on the United States, the whole world is buyin'. You know they gettin' 'em now. And rhythm and blues are just really spreadin' in the European market and industry. I don't think it's gonna die. I'm gonna try not to let it die.

I imagine there's all kinds of screams. Most screams that guys are doin' are off-key. Like James, he'll scream between the notes. He screams, but nobody never know what key he's in! But I scream on key. Like if I be singin' on a level, I will scream an octave higher in the same key. Man, that really tightens up those vocal chords and that stretches 'em. And if you're not used to it, you can hurt yourself. I'm used to it; I find I can do it with ease. It don't bother me. When I first started, I didn't just come out and do it; I gradually built up this thing. And I think if I hadn't've been a gospel singer all those years, I couldn't last singin' like I do. And I think the gospel field had a lot to do with that. It did. Definitely helped me, because it developed the kind of voice that I wanted to have. A real hard-type drivin' voice.

Wilson Pickett

Wilson Pickett

Sam & Dave

We never really began to work up an act because most of Sam and my things on the stage are original. We don't practice, rehearse, or nothin'. Just what comes up. What I feel like doin' I do, and what he feels like doin' he does. And that's it.

Dave Prater

Well, we like to get down sometime and get real home. We try . . . what we try to do is stay within the same trend as what we are—Sam & Dave—rather than try to take a song and sing it as the past artist did it. We might take that song and attack it a little differently than the past artist did. So this would still identify Sam & Dave their own traditional way.

Sam Moore

Jerry Butler

Jerry has his own style. They call him the Iceman 'cause he doesn't move, but he has soul. He doesn't have to move. This is his style, and everyone is entitled to their own style, and Jerry has his. He's just a soulful smooth singer and a very nice person. Like this is his thing. This is Jerry.

Yvonne Staples/The Staple Singers

When I started singing, everybody was jumpin' around. They were doing the splits and taking their clothes off and jumpin' off the stage and runnin' through the audience. I was never a good dancer. If I got on the stage with Jackie Wilson and James Brown, I had to get wiped out tryin' to dance. You know what I mean . . . you're onstage with these guys and say, "Get ready for this step I'm goin' to whip on you." It was just gonna come off like nothin'. I never wanted to be that type of performer. Nat Cole was my idea of the class thing, man. I've always wanted to be that. I've always wanted to walk out, to make my statement, to take my bow and to split. I never wanted to be jumpin' up and downsville. I didn't want things to get too exciting. I wanted to be able to control the situation. I didn't want it to get out of hand. Which is what happens when you get that kind of vibration going. You get it up there and you can't control it. You don't know what the audience is gonna do. You don't know

Sam Moore

what you're going to do. You don't know what's going to happen. Which is a lot of the reasons why there used to be riots and stuff like when James and all them perform because the people, at this point, they were in a frenzy and anything could happen. I never wanted to be in that kind of thing. I always wanted to be able to control. Because, like, this may sound weird, but I like playing with the emotions. I want to be able to make a person sad and then lead him out of that sadness and make him smile, make him happy. And then to take him back to it—where it's more than just complete laughter or complete tears or complete anything. I just want variety. And because I was a stand-up singer and because that was the way I wanted my thing to be, a disc jockey started to use the word "cool." But "cool" was like everybody was usin' it. So then it went to "supercool," which was just "cool" with another word added on to it. Finally it resolved itself into "the Iceman," which he thought was like the total statement about who I was. And it stuck. People picked it up. And with him like being the biggest disc jockey in Philadelphia at that time, it was kind of the normal thing to happen. Then it kind of drifted, and people that know me, know me as the Iceman.

Jerry Butler

Issac Hayes

Isaac Hayes is a monster! You ought to listen to this album he has out. Isaac Hayes is a monster! He's tall, dark, and bald! And he can sing!

Sam Moore/Sam & Dave

The Isley Brothers

Now we're trying to establish a certain type of sound with our music. And not just the band banging things out. Like we separate every instrument so that the instrument—rhythm section, guitars, and so forth—can say just what the song is saying.

Ronnie Isley

"It's Your Thing" was really the beginning of our thing. It carried a message. And the message was, "It is your thing," meaning us relating to other people, that whatever you want to do, whatever goal, whatever idea you have in mind, it is yours, you know. "Do what you want to do/I cannot tell you/Who to sock it to" . . . when to do it, how to do it, where to do it, why you should do it. And I think that this was one of the main reasons that this record sold over two million copies, because everybody accepted it as their own thing. That makes us feel very, very good—that you can relate a message of what you feel and for other people to accept it as theirs. And that's how that came about.

Kelly Isley

The Rascals

FUSION: ROCK AND SOUL

The Rascals

We started more or less together. And the reason we have stayed together, I think, is because we have a certain respect for each other. We're completely different from each other. That has a lot to do with it. Nobody tries to be like the other guy, because the other guy is so far removed from you, you know. So this is kind of how we do it: We have like certain lines that we draw where other people don't intrude in. And the common goal or the name of the group is what constitutes our relationship. Privately we don't interfere with each other. This makes a big difference. When we first started, we all used to live in the same—I won't call it a house, because it wasn't really a house—it was more like a jungle. We all lived in the same jungle, and it was fun. It was really good in those days. But naturally when people grow, people mature, and ideas change and you have to draw some kind of line.

It's almost like being married, but three times to three very funny-looking guys—four of us. But, no, there's a guy in the group by the name of Eddie

Brigati who's like . . . I think he's the funniest guy on earth. When he gets going, he's . . . like he keeps us laughing in the greatest of difficulties. Like on the road when we just broke down, you know, he's funny, and it's really a tremendous help. It really is. I can remember times like when for example we did a Dick Clark tour, which is like I'm sure that anybody you speak to about it will have the same reaction to it. It's like "Oh, God, have mercy." But we broke down and we had stomachaches from laughing because like it was so silly what he was doing. He was trying to hitch, you know, get attention, but he felt nobody would stop unless he started to take off his clothes. You know? No, really. It's a big difference being able to laugh at yourself . . . is a very healthy thing.

Around that same period that "People Got To Be Free" happened, we did a concert with a group, Young/Holt, and we were talking to them, and they were telling us that they really dug the opportunity of playing with us because normally they don't get to play for white people. And it suddenly dawned on me that a lot of black acts are not getting a chance to be heard by the white people, and vice versa. A lot of white acts don't get a chance to be heard by black people because they feel as if they

Isaac Hayes

are not welcome at a show if the whole show is black. So we decided that, number one, we could help the issue by integrating. Number two, we would have a better time when we were playing because black people seem to get into the music a little differently. And number three, we could groove on whoever was there performing with us. So it turned to be . . . everything turned to be fine.

Felix Cavaliere

Santana

I would just say Santana is a melody of rhythms, not melody and rhythms, because the rhythm is the major thing that's going on right now. We're changing things now, but like the rhythm thing is what we really got into. And there's not a lot of melody although there is if you really listen. Just like in jazz. A lot of people say there's no melody there, but there really is.

Two and a half years ago we used to play blues and we had a conga drummer. I don't know why we had a conga drummer really, except that we liked the sound of it and what it could do in some songs. But then it evolved that we liked those songs better than the blues.

I'm from Palo Alto, California. Mike here is from Redwood City. Chepito is from Nicaragua. Carlos is from Mexico. Mike, the conga drummer, is from San Francisco. David's from Texas and Daly City, and who knows where. We're not sure if his name is David Brown. Santana is Carlos's last name.

In San Francisco there's a bunch of beaches where conga drummers just go and play. And the conga drummer that we had first said, "I'd like to do 'Jingo' except with music." So, okay, and we listened to Olatunji who put it out—"Jingoloba"—and really got into what it was and what it was supposed to do, and then we just played to it.

Greg Rolie and Mike Shreive

Fred, Sly and Larry

Sly and the Family Stone

He's a very good songwriter. "Dance to the Music" is a nice song. The way it's put together is why it happened. As songs themselves, they're nice. They're actually funk bubble gum in a way, but the arrangements are sensational, you know . . . how he works out those things. That's good.

Jerry Ragovoy

Sly's my idea of a beautiful group. They get me off. Like very few people get me off as a group, as a total thing. No individual cat, but as a total thing. They really get me off.

Marty Balin/Jefferson Airplane

Now I dig me some Sly and the Family Stone! I dig them 'cause they're into a familylike thing, the same kind of thing that we are, that we've been down through the years. And like the rest of 'em aren't—he has his brother and sister in there—the rest of 'em aren't his relatives, but they're so tight, they know where each other's going. He can hit something, and they know. Just like daddy can hit something and we know where daddy's going. If Cleetie goes one way, I know where she's going, and we say that same phrase that same way. If it's in a background and she go up, I go up, too, and we come back down at the same time. Sly and them,

Santana

the first time I heard them when they did "Dance to the Music," I could tell they were straight from church. You know, I could tell! 'Cause when they go "dum-dum-dum—dumdumdum . . ." that's just a thing, and they had the tambourine in there. It was just something about them. From that song I wanted to see them, see who they were, what they looked like. I tried to picture them in my mind, how they looked, and then I happened to see them on television one day. And I said, "Well, that's them. Umhum!" I could see that they were young people. I knew it was a young sound. From that record on, I dug them. And everything they do . . . you know, a lot of people just look at a lead singer in groups like that . . . but all of 'em—they're just together. Everybody plays a part. Everybody is like a leader. You know Sly *is* the leader. Everybody's not like a leader, but they do their own thing.

Mavis Staples/The Staple Singers

Sly and the Family Stone—I think they're pure unadulterated funk. I call them funk, funk, funk!

Sly and the Family Stone are everyday people. That's beautiful. We are all everyday people. We all work hard. Some of us will never reach the goal financially that we wanted to reach, but we're happy because we're everyday people.

Little Richard

I really admire Sly. Sly can get all the dynamics, man. He can cool you out and he can bring you up to an amazing height without getting tasteless or boisterous about it. If he is boisterous, it's in a good way, and you can still hear. And, man, there's always that energy. There's an energy level. He can quiet it down, but you still feel that energy. There's somebody who has really captured the whole thing. Nothing but accolades for Sly, really! They are scary.

Spencer Dryden/Jefferson Airplane

Cynthia

Rose

By Sly's stuff not following a particular pattern, you don't never know what he's goin' to do next. I think this is why they dig him so much, because the younger generation is that way. You don't know what they goin' to do next. They're just free and wide open, and that's the way his music is. I dig Sly because he still has a message. It's not just a wild sound like they're just doin' anything, and just noise. That's why I dig Sly, because he tells a message along with his thing.

Gladys Knight and the Pips

William and Edward and I recorded some tunes for a record company that were like in this particular bag that Sly is in today, but the man that owned the record company was afraid to release it. He said, "Hey, that's too weird for me now. I can't go for it." That's why I like Sly and the Family Stone so much because they came up with the idea and they really put it into operation, and you see where they are now. I love the group. It's beautiful to me.

Mereld Knight

Sly is fascist rock or real demogogue rock. He is working with a mob. He leads everyone to the cathartic reactions that were at the beginning of rock and roll. It's a real challenge to white music, which is just strolling around on stage saying, "It's just my music and dig it."

Audience

Yes, yes, yes, yes . . . "Hot Fun in the Summertime." He's unbelievable.

Jerry Butler

I think it's because even if people can't because of their own hang-ups or inhibitions, even those people that cannot get into what they would like to get into on account of that, they somehow find room in "Higher and Higher" to feel like they're letting it all hang out without blowing anything. It puts the house shoes on people who really want to put house shoes on but don't want nobody else to know it!

"Somebody's Watching You"—you know why? 'Cause I've seen a lot of things when somebody thought that nobody was watching. Really. Then I've done a lot of things when I thought nobody was watching, and I believe somebody really was, 'cause I remember when I was watching and somebody thought nobody was watching. You know what I mean? If no more than somebody ridin' in a cab, playin' with their nose. I've seen that: I saw a chick doin' that right outside here. I was in a cab and she was in a limousine playin' with her nose, and she was tryin' to be sneaky. So if it's like that, somebody really must be watchin'. Like there ain't nobody gettin' away with nothin'! Everybody knows what's goin' on. That's how come there's a balance of things. 'Cause there's always somebody knowin' how to get rid of *that,* and that gets rid of that, and that gets rid of that. Ain't no secrets anymore.

Sly Stone

Joe Cocker

Joe Cocker and the Grease Band

It first caught my interest when I was fifteen. It really caught the whole of me like that. I was really into rock and roll and all the counterpart. I never thought about wanting to do anything else. I was a gas fitter, you know, for quite a while, 'bout five years, which was a good insight in some ways. You used to go around people's houses, meet a lot of people. But still every night we used to be out playin'. I never really stopped long enough to figure out why. I was learning to sing. It was just compulsive.

There are, you know—I get black guys coming up and saying they enjoyed the show. A lot of them are very skeptical about what the whole thing's about, 'specially when somebody's from England, which seems a bit of a strange country to a lot of Americans.

It must be about four years ago when I had me a group and I just read some articles by Jimmy Smith, talking about somebody having a lot of grease. I've never heard it used in connection for that word, for soul or anything. So I thought that sounds . . . there were too many people calling themselves soul bands and all this stuff. I mean it just seemed a bit out to me, so I called it Joe Cocker's Grease Band. But everybody sort of took it the wrong way and used to go ughhh!

It's really weird because there's not that many songs I actually like. I buy a lot of records just to give them a casual listen, and if anything sticks, that's why I end up doing the stuff. Dylan and the Beatles' songs are so strong you can move them about; you can tilt or twist them around, and they still hold fast. There's not that many songs I can really sing these days, and that's why we really got to start concentrating on writing songs. . . .

There was a stage of life when I sang all blues. I was Muddy Waters and sort of got into this thing. I suddenly thought to myself, "Well, this is a kid idea, you know—just trying to sing the blues, the twelve-bar blues forever." I mean, singing that just didn't seem right. Everybody happens to go through different things. You just try and pick up on what's going around you at the time and it seeps into the music.

Joe Cocker

Dr. John, the Night Tripper

I love Dr. John's albums. He really is funky. He's just so funky. There's just something really appealing and earthy about it. It's different. I guess it's basically blues, but it's done differently. Completely his own thing.

Johnny Winter

My music is influenced by music from around Louisiana. It's Cajun, Creole, and it's influenced by a lot of music. You know all music is influenced by other music. My music is influenced by music from around that part of the country.

Dr. John

Just one costume. Everything is one. Everything boils down to one. Everything is hittin' on one. Start separatin' things into five . . . it gets confusing. It all represents one: me. It's you, too. It's within you. It's within me. It's just one God. It's just one me. Just one within. You got to be one with yourself, like you know they say in the Bible: you have to be in season in order to catch the right season when it come, you have to be in order. That's what it boils down to. That's basic.

Words to me are just the sound of the voice. And the words don't have all the meaning to 'em, 'cause somebody could say the same thing a different bunch of ways and meanings. Words don't really explain it all.

I believe that God is the supreme thinker and we are like trying to get away from his thoughts. Like God has a set of paths for us to follow . . . like I believe in the Bible. I was raised on the Bible. I believe in it more thoroughly than any book I've read. Be it ever so humble, there's no book like the Bible to me. They say it's easier to go a side path than it is to go a straight path. To me a church should be a place where poor people can go to rest. It shouldn't be no place where people got to dress up to go to church. That's sick. Poor people should be able to go to sleep in a church. That should be a rest haven. It should be God's house for the people that don't have no other house. Not where you put on your Sunday best to go to church. I get irritated by this. I get mad at everybody.

I think that the only way we can find what our purpose is in life, 'cause everybody's got a purpose, everybody's got a reason for being here, and the only way you can find it is by doin' what we're doin' right now, sit down and talk and sit down and don't hide from it. Don't hide from it. Right now you find everybody will hide behind dope, behind alcohol, behind television, any one of these things, rather than give yourself a good talkin' to sometimes. Do some soul-searchin' within yourself. Sit down, and I think everybody should have group therapies, like families or whatever groups people live in, man. Instead of just sittin' down and complimentin' and lyin' to each other and sayin' you're okay in my book, and when you turn around, you stab him in the back. It should be that—we should all sit down and criticize one another up front. And just say, well, look, you're wrong. Or I think you're crazy; you're really off the base. And say these kind of things, and each of us criticize the other one to help each other, 'cause the way things is, I can sit here and tell you. . . .

Dr. John, the Night Tripper

MC 5

Our program is makin' people have a good time. And we're gettin' closer and closer to the point where we'll be able to put that program into heavy use. All this summer we've been in the studio for four months doin' our album. Durin' the time we've been in the studio, our music has undergone some radical changes. We've just been makin' it tighter, writin' it tighter, and performin' it tighter, and practicin' more. We're just bein' more precise about it, and what's good, we're keepin' and expanding on. What was the excess, man, the flab, we're eliminating. Just bringing it all up to date.

We were into playin' for kids from the beginning. Because we were never into it for the money definitely because there was no money, the money comes later. But that's what we like to do; we like to play for kids. But the thing is we still like to play for kids, but we want to play for more kids because we feel that our music is goin' through a change, and it's becoming happier. I think that's what people need right now.

Everything we do is aimed at moving 'em. Gettin' 'em up from sitting down. You can feel it. Makin' 'em feel good. . . . There haven't been any bands playin' hot enough music for the people to get up and dance.

In the first place we're not really talkin' about going back to no old-fashioned sound. The thing that you want to get out of that old material is the energy and resensify it: the reality, real-to-life experience; super real-to-life in the lyric and in the reality of the energy of the music, the body movingness in old rock and roll, in soul music, like new black jazz. We do "Back in the U.S.A." and "Tutti Frutti" on the record. We're not tryin' to copy Little Richard or Chuck Berry. That's just ridiculous. That's nowhere. What we want to get is the life and energy out of that music and apply it in a contemporary context, apply the thing that will help our people today.

MC 5

Delaney and Bonnie and Friends, Featuring Eric Clapton

I perform because I really have fun. I really enjoy it. That's my whole idea of—they've labeled it now—swamp rock. But all I've ever done was try and take rock-and-roll music and some nice lyrics to it and make it happy instead of sad. I think sad songs are pretty, and once in a while I like to write a sad song, but ninety percent of my songs are happy songs, because I just think there's not enough happiness floatin' around.

Lately we've been getting great audiences. I don't know if that's because they sense we're havin' a good time, or they're havin' a good time, or we're all havin' a good time together. I hope that's what it is. When somebody feels like hollerin' I think they should holler. Because if they don't, they're not goin' to be completely fulfilled inside. If you feel like screamin' you should scream, you know, holler "Whoopee! Whoopee!" That's the kind of audience I like. They're free enough within theirself not to be ashamed to holler or let out a little emotion in front of their neighbor. That's the kind of crowd I like to play with. Black audiences are very good audiences about that. They're not ashamed of being emotional. They let it be known.

I think people should think about their music a little more than they do. Music is a form of entertainment and it should be left alone. And it's a great happy form—communication between people, you know. You should use it for a happy form of communication. I think it's gettin' back more that way. I think it's gettin' back to where if you got somethin' to say, you can say it, but there are some things, it seems like, it abuses music to sing about, to me. I really like my music. I like music a lot. I like everybody's music.

Delaney Bramlett

Eric Clapton and Friends

Bonnie and Delaney

Keith and Pete

THEATER ROCK

The Who

I was known as the quiet one of the group, and I sort of stood about, and there's no use trying to get rid of it now even though I'm not quiet. We all used to cater when we first started as a teeny-bopper group in England six years ago. We all used to cater for different parts of the audience. Like Keith would cater for the young girls who were like sort of potty about the way he looked. He doesn't look like that now, but they were potty about the way he looked like a little boy, and they went mad about him. And Roger sort of catered like for the girls a little bit older with "Oh, he's my idol," but with sex on their brains. And Pete catered for the intellectuals who didn't care that he had a big nose, but they thought he was a fantastic musician, and he had a good brain. And I used to cater for the older audience who were a little bit too cool to scream so they sat right at the back. So all the time they were going, "Oh, Roger!" "Keith!" and a few people were shouting, "Pee-tah!" And like all mine were at the back, deadly quiet, going, "Oh, he's very good, isn't he? He's very good." But I could never see any of this. I could only see the first two rows. I got such a complex about it. I mean you really build up complexes when you're in a group of four, and it seems that you're the most unpopular member. I mean you think, "What can I do? What can I do? Shall I . . . ?" But then you realize that your audience is a different audience completely. It's at the back and they don't scream. Once you realize that, it's okay. But for two years I was . . . I used sort of to have complete paranoia about being thrown out of the group because I wasn't good enough, you know.

The first two years were pretty violent years anyway. We were always fighting with each other. We are four different personalities. We're completely different. But we get on with each other because we know each other now. When we first started we'd been thrown together. When we made the first record we realized we had to stay together and we hated each other, because we wouldn't go out of our way to understand how the other person thought . . . most likely how most groups break up nowadays. We were very lucky. We were just about to break up when we had a number-one hit with "My Generation," so we had to stay together. And after that, for the next eighteen months, every record that we released went up in the Top 5. And we thought, "Oh, well, as we're here for keeps we might as well get to know each other." And what with starting American tours and being thrown together—in the beginning sleeping in the same room—I mean you just have to get to know the other person, which is why we've lasted this long.

John Entwistle

Pete Townshend

Bonzo Dog Band

The Bonzo Dog Band started off as a vaudeville band, and for years they used to do a television show every week called "Do Not Adjust Your Set." It was a comedy thing. They used to sing in that sort of style. They went through all that scene, and they realized that that was going to get them nowhere, so they changed to rock and roll. They did that "Magical Mystery Tour" thing, and then people sort of realized that they changed to rock and roll. They sang like Hound Dog on that. They've done incredible shows at universities that we've actually played with them, and we've stayed there, just splittin' our sides. They're all exactly the same offstage—completely insane.

John Entwistle/The Who

Bonzo Dog Band

Tina Turner

Tina Turner

Us women have come a long way. But on our way up we changed a little bit, and I don't mean changin' tires on trucks and drivin' bulldozers and things. I mean we've changed as far as wantin' some of the same things you men want. You fellas are possessive. You want what's yours to be yours. That's what us women want. You better not think you're sharin' your old lady with nobody else. Well, now we don't want to feel that we're sharin' you with nobody else. Now, you fellas think because you're a man you can do a lot of things and get by with it and you say us women are supposed to understand. Some of you fellas have the knack of sayin', "Well, I'm a man and a woman just can't do what a man do." Then of course you have some of those fellows that's players. You know a lot of you men think that you can tell us women anything. Ike tells me, "Well, how am I going to know

what I got at home if I can't test what's out there in the streets?"

The players say, "Well, no matter what I do there in the streets, I'm goin' to always take care of home." Well, you cool, you cool. It's true that most of you men do take care of home. But us women know that you're takin' care of some more homes, too. That just goes to show you that this saying here is very true: the downfall of a lot of good men is the upkeep of too many women. But I want to ask you this. This is somethin' that I've been wanting to know for a little while: fellas, while you're out there in the streets havin' so much fun, did you ever stop to think what was goin' on at home? Ha-ha-ha! You better think about it. But I'm going to ask you this now because I want to know who, I want to know, who, whoooo . . . I said I want to know, I want to know who's makin' love to your old lady while you were out makin' love.

I'm gonna let you go, but I just want to say that you fellas have got it made, you know. Because, you see, a man can make his woman whatever he wants her to be. That's, of course, if she's a woman. But the problem is that most of the time he ain't never satisfied. He's too busy thinkin' about what's out there in the streets he can get. But, fellas, you've started us women to thinkin.' Yeah, we can think, too. And we think, too. And we think that whatever's out there in the streets must be good! 'Cause you fellas've been out there a long time! Now us women want to go out there and get us some, too. And now I, I want you to stay where you are, 'cause, as I said before, I'm goin' to talk about some music, some soulful music. All music has soul, 'cause everybody has soul. Everybody has a soul and if you do your best and you put your soul into it, it's soulful.

The kind of soul I'm talkin' about has got the grease. Ain't nothin' no good without the grease. Ha-ha. Right now. I want to see if you can find the groove, and it's greasy, soulful music. Hey!! That's what I call soul music! I want everybody to get together now and I want you to do it! And now get it. And do the soul clap, you all. Clap your hands. Everybody! Clap your . . . clap your hands, everybody!"

Tina Turner

Tina Turner

Jim Morrison

The Rock World

ROOTS: GOSPEL

We all come from the church. I can honestly say that most of my talents were developed in the church, as well as finding that I did have a little gift in being able to create. Fred and Sam, we all at one time sang with different gospel groups and, of course, that goes as well for Sam Cooke, Aretha Franklin, Temptations. So there is a definite similarity there which I would imagine you would call soul.

Curtis Mayfield/ The Impressions

Since I was three I played in church. I first played in the church for my mother. I used to play for revivals, all the choirs, Sunday school, BYPU. Do you know what BYPU is? (Baptists' Young People's Union).

Well, that's an experience. At the revival meetings when the music gets very intense . . . they have the same thing in Africa . . . when it gets very intense and it reaches everybody, you can just lose your mind 'cause it's so hypnotic. You can almost feel it in the room. My mother used to say, "One day the whole world is coming around to this." She has said it since I can remember. And I'm just so glad that she's lived long enough to see it. That's how I feel. Because not only didn't I believe her, at that time I was slightly ashamed of it. But she knew.

She even knew that it would come to pass where makeup as we used to know it wouldn't be used. My mother knew! And she's known all her life. My mother's something else! But she's a very religious and spiritual person. She lives in that, you know. She's a very deeply religious person.

Nina Simone

Some people say gospel delivering is more of a message than any spiritual. But this is not my feeling. The way I feel about gospel, spiritual, rock and roll, and all of it, is one of the same. The difference— we're saying Jesus on songs and they're saying baby, so really and truly to me there's really no difference.

Now, I've heard people giving definitions on it and gospel would be, like I would consider "Precious Lord" a spiritual but gospel would be something like "Marching up to Zion."

Yvonne Staples/The Staple Singers

"A World of Darkness," "Hey Jude" or "Funky Broadway," or the type thing that Wilson Pickett is doing—that's from a spiritual bag. That's where I come from. I came from the church. I was a minister at fourteen. I was a minister for two years. I sung spirituals for about ten years. And at seventeen I went into rock and roll, at that time. You don't have to sing spirituals to believe in the church or Christ or whatever you believe in. So when I came to that, that's when I did it.

I've sung spirituals for years and years. I've sung in New York City in 1955 before I ever thought about going in the Apollo Theater. The people that I see now that I'd known when I was younger and singin' spiritual, they come to see me now. This is like a thirteen-year relationship. What I did in the last five years with the Temptations, that's not where my career came from. My career came from Mavis, the Dixie Nightingales, the Dixie Hummin' Birds, Swan Silvertone Singers. I didn't just start singin' with the Temptations. I've been singin' a long time.

David Ruffin

I was singing in church about fifteen years. It started out what we had to do really. I probably wouldn't have gone to church that much, but my mother and father were kind of strict. They laid it down. And we were to follow. There was no running away. They'd come and get us and bring us back, and we still had to do it, you know. That kind of thing. They are really religious.

It's called the Church of God in Christ. Some people call it Holy Roly. You can feel it when you walk in. Sit there awhile. As soon as you lose, if you have any, fear of . . . not fear. As soon as you can relax, then the thing that's there will take over, and it'll just take you, and there you go. They believe in lettin' it all hang out!

It was church up until the time I played in a nightclub. And after I played in a nightclub, you couldn't play in church any longer. I could have, but I really didn't feel like getting those crossed up. But now I think it would be all right. You see, I feel different about that now. I think we should be able to sing church songs and all kinds of songs . . . any . . . truth songs, anywhere. Truth is good for anybody.

Sly Stone/Sly and the Family Stone

Country Joe & the Fish

The Staple Singers

The whole family are responsible for so much influence upon other people. I have about six of their albums. Mavis is a great stylist. There's a warmth.

John Kay/Steppenwolf

Whew! That girl, man! Mavis! She kills me. The whole family are beautiful.

Dave/Sam & Dave

I think Mavis is on the top floor. I like how she uses her voice. She never seems to go that far out of it that she loses control.

Joe Cocker

Oh, man, Mavis sings, and I just . . . wooooo! What a voice! Fantastic voice. They want me to write them a song. I'm really anxious to try something. She's so good, wow.

Felix Cavaliere/The Rascals

Rock and roll has taken gospel and made hits just by changin' a few words and keepin' the same beat and harmony as we use. I know that's where it's at, so that's why I'm gonna stay with gospel. The main thing we try to do is get the younger people to listen to what we're sayin'.

Pop Staples

The Staple Singers

Dave Prater

Edwin Hawkins

Any musical piece I've ever worked with I've always wanted to be just a little bit different than just a regular gospel number. Some of the people in church say that the music sounds a little worldly, or it sounds like pop, or a little too jazzy for gospel music, but if they really realize or remember some years back that all of this music originated from the church in the beginning, it just so happens that you had some musicians that maybe studied music and they organized it in a way that they thought sounded sacred. But this doesn't necessarily make it gospel music . . . just because it sounds sacred. And gospel music is to be a lively music anyhow because God is not dead. He's alive!

You have people everywhere searching for something, and some of them don't know what they're searching for. I really believe that they are looking for God and don't know it. And they're all these different trips, but I'm happy to tell them that Jesus is the only trip. He's the only trip. He's the one that you don't have to come off of.

Edwin Hawkins

Little Richard

ROOTS: ROCK AND ROLL

Little Richard

I go up high. Yes . . . from the diaphragm . . . all the way. That's when you be so strong, because I have a support when I go up.

I got that from the church. I used to sing in church, really, and you know, you sing a religious song and then you make that high note. That's where I got it.

The church is the foundation and then from the foundation I . . . it sprang out and you go forth into all parts of the world. You got something to tell. You knew about love all the time, but you got a power to help your delivery.

To teach happiness instead of sadness, instead of teaching prejudice, segregation, to teach togetherness. That we are all one, that we are all here for one purpose; we're all on the stage of life. And we must be good actors or we would disappoint God very much.

Rock and roll? The true ones are going to stay in it. The fakes and phonies have to fall down by the wayside because the road is too strong for them to walk. But it's your life. Like me, show business is my life. I've dedicated my whole entire life to it. All of it, yeah. Beautiful.

I've given that, so I'm supposed to do it. And money or no money, I'm supposed to do it. Yeah, black or white, brown, red, or whatever color, I'm supposed to do it. Because I believe we're all God's bouquet, the bouquet of love . . . all nations.

The white kids like my type beat. My type beat . . . they get their groove, and I get my groove there, too. If I didn't I couldn't sing it. I haven't had a record in ten years, and the market have proved their loyalty, their devotion, their appreciation to me, and they made me a legend, thank God for them. And they're still buying my records. And when I sing them, it's just as though I just recorded them yesterday. And I, I really dig that quite a bit.

Some people say that the power was green power. I must say that without green power you can't make it, but you need love power to handle green power.

Little Richard

I didn't know Little Richard sang gospel before he sang pop. We went down in Huntsville, Alabama. We had a program down there, and Richard came and told us he was goin' to the seminary and he was goin' to preach. He had cut his hair off, and he looked good with his hair cut like that!

Mavis Staples/ The Staple Singers

Little Richard, man, was the God! I grew up on Little Richard.

Marty Balin/Jefferson Airplane

I feel that I'm an ambassador of peace and goodwill. I'm not teaching people to hate. I'm not teaching people to steal. I'm not teaching black supremacy and neither am I teaching white supremacy. I'm teaching love, that all men are men, all men have red blood, all men was put here by God. And we are just like a big bouquet in the garden—like the sunflowers, the rose, the lilies, and the medallions. We are God's bouquet. All races belong to God. And can't nobody help what color they are. All men are proud of what they are.

I'm a conductor of revivals, the only minister in the whole package. Little Richard the evangelist.

I've been playing an audience, and like sometimes it's a hypnotic spell comes over the people. I seen it happen. I've seen people just leap out of their seats! It's deeper than excitement.

I can't dance, but give me the microphone and the piano, I'll rock your soul.

I call it the healing music, the music that makes the blind see, the lame, the deaf and dumb hear, walk, and talk. The music of joy, the music that uplifts your soul. I said, because I am the living flame, Little Richard is my name. I'm not conceited either. I'm convinced of the facts that the music is the real rock. Somebody said, "Well, Richard, rock and roll is just a lot of noise." I said, "Oh, no, no, no, no. It's not just a lot of noise. The same beat that you play in Bach you hit in rock!"

Little Richard

Little Richard was in Detroit and he was saying something about him being somewhere with Jerry Lee Lewis: "Don't miss this! If you miss this, you're going to miss the greatest thing that ever happened to you in your life. Come out and see us, honey! I wouldn't kid you." He was doing more plugging than the deejay was. He's just unbelievable.

Martha Reeves

Bob Dylan

Dylan's his own person. I must say, I am very proud of my people and our music. This to me is like something else. It gives me the essence of what I am. Out of the white musicians through the years that I have seen, the one—and I'm not talkin' about the formal, classical, 'cause that's a lot of technique blah-blah-blah, European music—Bob Dylan is the closest thing to a saint that I know of among white people in America. I feel this way about the man. He transcends color or anything that I might otherwise feel about it. And I'm glad to be able to say this. I don't think he has anything to do with it. What I'm talkin' about has nothing to do with him. It has to do with that "other thing" that he possesses. I really take my hat off to the man. I can think of many colored people that I think are saints, very few musically that are white, really, that are their own person, that come through in their own thing.

That man's had a lot of pain. That man's been through a lot of pain in his mind, in his head. He's been a lot of places. And he's able to say it. He lives outside the prejudices, etcetera. And I'm not talking about colored people, because to me they are obvious: Ray Charles and so many of them that are just geniuses. I secretly all these years haven't had very much respect for white people in their music because most of it is just not bein' anything. Really! He has this timelessness. You should be very proud of that man.

Nina Simone

When I look at these last three or four years the name that really hits me as far as writing is Bob Dylan. He kind of like—pow. I mean he opened up the whole field for everyone. Well, after you've been where he's been, it doesn't even matter. Most people never even get to that doorway, you know. He's really had a lot of influence on the music world.

Felix Cavaliere/The Rascals

Dylan's things do work. They shouldn't actually. Some of them just teeter; some of the things like "Gates of Eden" and things where they're really kind of overloaded images you would imagine somehow wouldn't work and do. It's a kind of magic that he's got, that makes it work. I don't think anybody else could.

Adrian Henri/The Liverpool Scene

I consider Dylan a great poet.

The Beatles were influenced by Dylan, but you asked me who influenced me, and I would never have, ever have heard Dylan if it hadn't been for the Beatles. So I've still got to put it all at their door.

They were a tremendous break in England, because they came over, got into the Dylan thing, and sort of came back and said, "Well, you ought to hear this guy Dylan." And all of the kids said, "Well, if the Beatles say we've got to listen to this guy, then we better get his records."

I think Dylan's responsible for lyrics becoming more meaningful. But at the same time I believe that the Beatles were looking for a way to make meaningful lyrics. If you look into their work even before Dylan, you can find them trying to emerge—proper lyricwise—which is the very reason they picked up on Dylan. Because, bang, he was a cat who was nothing else but lyric.

His recent sound, though . . . he's getting his voice together. In that—the *Nashville Skyline* album—he's actually singing. Before he was just sort of shouting it out.

Moody Blues

We like Bob Dylan's material because it is in keeping with the times. We admire him very much. His songs carry a message. This is what the Staple Singers is about. We want to get a message across, and we thought that those were good songs to sing and that's why we recorded them. You can see the things that are happenin' in those lyrics. You can actually see what's happenin', what he's sayin'. Like the song "John Brown"; "Oxford Town"—we've been down there in Oxford, Mississippi.

Dylan's an inspirational singer to me, though he is classed as a folk singer. His message is truth; he is true gospel as anything you would ever see.

A thing about Bob . . . he says just what should be said in a song. There's not a prejudiced bone in him, and he sees everybody as a person, regardless of color or anything.

The Staple Singers

Nina Simone

The Beatles

Elvis Presley doing what he did became the hero. The Beatles, the way they were accepted here in the States . . . sure, when they first started recording they did commercial music, like their first big hit record in England was "Twist and Shout," a carbon copy of our record. We did a million and a half records here in the States. They did five million worldwide.

Then they were able to say, "Let's really write; let's stop with the doo-wahs and whatever the people say is bad, and if they want serious things, let's really give 'em what they want and give 'em what we feel." And they came up with songs like "Yesterday," "Michelle," "Nowhere Man," "Eleanor Rigby" . . . you know, great tunes.

Now they had the audience who loved 'em, who cried, who pulled their hair out. They began to listen; adults began to listen. Because all the time that your parents are downstairs when you are upstairs, you know, they're listening. Like a child is listening when we think that we have the doors closed. They're listening, too. So I think that this made the change. It's a funny thing here in the States, how we are first with a lot of things, you know, and then bandwagon on some other things because we have great artists right here in the States. Not only with Elvis Presley, we had Bob Dylan writing message songs years ago before the Beatles.

Kelly Isley/The Isley Brothers

The Beatles came on like Camille (the hurricane), you know. They were an overnight sensation type thing, causing a lot of attention from the black kids who heretofore had not even really thought of the white artist as such on this scale. Not even Elvis Presley or any of these people got this kind of action from the black kids. You dig? Consequently, I think with them coming over and having such a great influence for the first time on the black youth, and making the statements that they made pertaining to who they had dug and where they had got their thing from, the black people that they had really started their own sound from, it brought a lot of attention to the black artist from the white youth. You dig? So I would say that music today is definitely the greatest bridge that people have. I mean, it has done more for racial relationships, especially among young people, than any other thing, any of the laws that they have enforced or anything that they've forced on people. It's just happening through music. The kids get together, doin' the same dances, they dig the same people now, which is a first in the music world. You dig? "I Want To Hold Your Hand" had to sell a million to black people, I'm sure.

You could take the Beatles to a predominantly black neighborhood, whereas if they went to a predominantly white neighborhood, they would be completely enthralled and mobbed. I mean, there would be no question about it, they wouldn't have any clothes on or no arms or legs or what have you. And you could take the Beatles and bring 'em down here, and although the kids would come and check 'em out and dig 'em, you know, it wouldn't be the excitement thing that it would be in a white neighborhood because of the fact that they do not yet feel close enough to them to do this thing. Whereas they would give it to James Brown or a black artist. They would do the same thing to him as the white kids would to the Beatles.

The Beatles actually are not the loud, loud rock group. The Beatles, as you know, have done some great soft songs. Some of the greatest songs ever done were done by these guys: John Lennon and Paul McCartney. They are not the real loud, loud rock group. The Beatles are not as loud as the Stones.

Smokey Robinson

There was no work in the early sixties at all. That's somethin' the Beatles really changed. Like the only place we could ever expect to play would be like in high school for the high school. And then when we got out of high school, there was no place to play. For about a year, really. It was after that year that the Beatles came along, and suddenly people started having dances and stuff again and hiring "live" bands, which was very unique before. We found ourselves in what looked like a dead-end trade, and the Beatles came and everybody wanted a band and everybody was in one. Like when we were in high school, we were the only people that even played music, I mean, rock. And we were the only band in the school. Now I guess every high school's got fifty or sixty of 'em. It's really strange.

Tom and John Fogerty/ Creedence Clearwater Revival

The marvelous thing about the Beatles is really very hard to appreciate in America. They've done a terrific lot to build up the confidence of people in the provinces. In doing their own thing in their own thing and not going to London to do it. In England there really is a thing about everything centered in London. And they eventually had to move there, and obviously they went there a lot to do recordings for business reasons. But they did stick out for quite a long time. In England, if you were a pop singer you always acquired a kind of Middle Atlantic accent and show biz manner and things. And they absolutely refused to do this. They never changed. They were always kind of Liverpool guys.

And this did a terrific lot in a very wide sense for things like poetry and things. So that suddenly everybody thought, well, maybe I can stay at home and do it instead of having to go to the big city and become a Londoner and talk like people in London. I can do my thing in my own place. So that sort of widespread effect has been terrific really.

They are very funny because there's so much you can say about them. It was amazing the way they had a fanatical local following before they ever recorded. I know girls who used to go and queue all night to sit in the front row at the Cavern . . . not to get in the Cavern, because there was no trouble getting in to see them until they got very, very popular. It was simply that it was a great honor to sit in the front row, and if you couldn't get the front row, you would get the second row. It wasn't a kind of groupie thing because it wasn't necessarily to do with sex at all. But they were just very ardent fans. They had a very kind of symbiotic sort of relationship. Because they knew all these girls by name, and they were all very nice. And those chicks were always terribly up-tight about all the girls screaming at them and things. Because that was a very uncool thing to do. You know, they shouldn't do that, they should listen, and all that.

And their fan club is still run by the girl from Liverpool who ran it before they started recording, which is kind of very nice.

Adrian Henri/The Liverpool Scene

The Kinks

I don't want people to forget we are a rock and roll band. I know this on the stage, but when we get in the studios and spend a bit of time there, it does tend to sort of simmer down a bit. We do other things as well. But onstage, we'll always be a rock and roll band. I never really thought about playing rock. It meant a solution to certain things and a way to express myself. I hate to sort of finish everything I'm ever gonna do and feel I haven't expressed anything. Yes, gotta do it.

Ray Davies/The Kinks

The Kinks' songs are somewhere in between sort of music hall things and straight rock music as you have it here in America. And it's great—sort of English songs that possibly don't come over here in the same way. "Sunny Afternoon" and "Walking in the Sunset"—all those things are just terribly about England. And maybe that's what I like and admire about them more than anything else. I think they're a very good act and that they are marvelous singers.

Adrian Henri/The Liverpool Scene

Ray Davies

Mick Jagger

The Rolling Stones

I thought we stood for infinity.

Mick Jagger

You have a personality such as Jagger. Here I see a man around my age, and the way he approaches his art is so similar really to the way that I would approach mine. But his method of expression is far looser than let's say I found in many of my contemporaries in classics. Whereas he would spend time with a recording session getting into himself and really, really feeling basic . . . basic feelings and feeling comfortable with himself and having unlimited time and this whole feeling of just feeling now . . . feeling how his whole inner being and his molding of his statement.

I think Jagger is more basically truthful than the Beatles. I just think that Jagger is more basically animal; he's more basically into those feelings; he is more basically concerned without going out and writing you-dirty-pig-cops type of lyric. He's very much in touch with himself. He's an artist.

Lorin Hollander

Mick Jagger is very vocal about what he believes. I've read a couple of things, an article and things that he has said, that are very, very conscious of what's going down. He is not by any matter of means an unpolitical person. A lot of his tunes get the English public very up-tight. They don't affect the Americans that way because we don't relate to them. Like that thing that he did—"Particular Habits." I understand it's a direct slam at the English bourgeoisie—you know, having tea at three in the afternoon and that whole trip. It's a big dump on 'em. The chicks in the audience here react to the line, "Would you like to live with me?" That was the big thing here, but that's not the big thing in the song. It seems to work, though.

But "Street Fighting Man" is an obvious thing that people on both sides of the Atlantic can relate to—right away. The same things are happening. People get hassled by the heat, there's absurd governmental hassles, and things like that. That's something that relates immediately; the "Particular Habits" thing doesn't.

Jorma Kaukonen/Jefferson Airplane

Chuck Berry

There's a real toughness of lyric in Chuck Berry's songs.

Adrian Henri/The Liverpool Scene

Chuck Berry was the first one to capture the cadence of American speech in song.

John Sebastian

Chuck Berry

Lonnie Mack

Lonnie Mack's another one of these guys that I really dig. Him and Taj Mahal. I dig Lonnie Mack for some of the same reasons that I dig Taj Mahal. In the first place he's a very strong musician. Also he sings well and he's the kind of guy that's been doing blues, R & B, and country for ten years. He did it way before it was hip to do it.

Elvin Bishop

Lonnie Mack

Grace Slick and Marty Balin

THE SONG

You don't think too much about it. One song can have three changes. Every song written is like a leaf on your tree of changes.

Donovan

I'm a song lover. First of all, the song is the most important thing.

If it's a good song, I dig it, as opposed to something . . . just a bunch of words scrambled up, which is happening a lot these days.

Smokey Robinson

In a song you have to obey certain rules of meter and rhyming, whereas in poetry you don't have to follow those rules of rhyme and rhythm.

Since I do not play a musical instrument, I must make up words as fast as I can to hold onto the melody that enters my mind. I use pen and paper, the physical act of writing. On a tape recording you eventually have to transcribe, and the sound of my own voice makes me self-conscious in composing.

Jim Morrison/The Doors

Music is all the same thing, whether it comes from India, the States, Greenland, Africa, Irish. It's all the same music, because it's just music. After I realized that, I started writing.

Stevie Winwood

If you're a writer, it's like makin' a sandwich. It really is. There's no great thing in it. The great thing is . . . if any writer makes complicated explanations for his work, "I do this, and then I put that together with it," he's full of shit! Because writing is a beautiful gift, and if you've got it, then you let everybody do it. "Hear, listen to this," and you're sharin' your song with everybody. And if you kept them and I made this song, your burden would be so heavy you wouldn't be able to walk. When you've written a song, you nip it off and you leave a tune. You've written it and enjoyed writing it. And you enjoyed people hearing it, but it's not yours anymore. It goes. So that simplicity you keep finding in people's work, it's that they get into a scene and they say, "Jazz, pop, folk, and put this and put that there and . . ." In the end they do all that, and the album is fantastic. They say, "Let's do something else. Well, what will we do? Well, there's nowhere else to go in that direction, so we'll just make songs again, you know, just simple." Until some other form comes along and stirs you up, like Indian did. The Beatles and everybody. Stirred everybody up. You get into it, but in the end Indian music is drone music. Every country's got drone music. It was sort of a fad.

Donovan

All of the songs that I've ever written have been inspired things. I used to travel with a tape recorder in case something came to mind that I didn't want to forget. And then that was so cumbersome I started to use association. Like I would try to associate whatever the melody was with a lyric or title or something. And most of the times I would only think of these things when I was traveling, driving a car or flyin' in a plane or something. If nobody bothered me, I could just keep hummin' it to myself until I stored it up in the back of my mind, and I could recall it whenever I wanted to.

Jerry Butler

I find it very easy to write the music once I've got the words. I've got thousands of tunes going around in my head that I could fit together if I could have the words first. Otherwise I just can't imagine them at all.

I can't stand plagiarism. If I've got something musical in my head that I've thought up and I think it sounds like anything else, I'll scrap it straight away. It's got to be something completely different. And I throw most of my material out—if it sounds like another number to me or it sounds a bit too much like the Rolling Stones or the Beatles, I'll scrap that. I suppose all my numbers have sort of a distinct style. I suppose that's how it's come about because I throw most of the other stuff out.

John Entwistle/The Who

I think lyrically you can pinpoint an experience, whereas instrumentally you can't pinpoint where this happened or what happened because it's a very physical thing and indefinite. When I write a song I remember the day and the time and the place, because often the song is about a day, a time, and a place. Once you start using words, it becomes tied down.

Barry Melton/Country Joe & the Fish

The writing sort of comes as a result of experiences that you are going through and it's spontaneous rather than planned. I mean, it either comes or it doesn't come. And the way I like to describe it is as if I was a tuner—a radio tuner—and I get to the right frequency and it just pours right through.

Felix Cavaliere/The Rascals

So many people today are writing and singing protest or songs with messages simply because for so long, commercially, through radio, they've been very oppressed by not being able to truly say in a whole lot of ways what they would like to say. If it wasn't rock and roll or pop songs or something with love and "shake your happy" a whole lot of ways, you were censored. Today everything is a bit more open. The Bob Dylans, all these type of people, have sort of opened the doors, and the public itself is just more down-to-earth as to being able to say, "Well, do your own thing. Whatever you got to say, say it. Whether I can accept it, dislike it, like it, you have the right to say it."

Curtis Mayfield/The Impressions

It's usually with me the music that comes first . . . a melody that starts to eat away at me over a period of time. I spend a lot of time at the piano trying to find things that knock me out. A lot of times extensions of those things become pieces of music. I'm into composition more than I am writing tunes.

Felix Pappalardi/Mountain

I got kind of a western music tune that came out of that grand source for many of us writers: the fantastic and amazing Holiday Inn! And it's strange, because it seems that an awful lot of my friends have ended up writing songs in Holiday Inns. Which goes to show you that the muse just ain't that choosy about where it happens as long as it happens.

Barry Melton

It's weird. The Spoonful, in the course of traveling in the early years, had a lot of time in those places and got into just sitting in those Holiday Inns. It's like . . . it's like being nowhere. No, but I mean, have you ever tried to imagine really like nothing? Have you ever tried to imagine nothing? I mean just that, incidentally. I mean, really, man, not like a, you know, kind of a cloudy gray nothing. Not like that sort of navy blue Hayden Planetarium style nothing. Can you imagine that? Close your eyes and try to just like focus on really just seeing nothing, and then down the center of all that nothing is a long road just goin' on as far as the eye can see. Then running down way on the horizon at the end of that road . . . and it's a Holiday Inn! We, like I say, we spent a lot of time there, and this particular tune, if I recall correctly, was written on the same day when I met a bagpipe player who just happened to be at Dayton, Ohio. I was sitting in my room, and all of a sudden I hear bagpipes outside. Well, he was playing a tune in the same key I was writing in. So I figured right, okay, just keep that up, just stay out there in the courtyard and keep doin' it. That was the key anyway.

John Sebastian

John Sebastian

Well, "Darkness" came to be written after a rather heavy emotional experience. I had been up all night thinking and talking and I had a bad thought and talked and felt everything that I could. I wanted to go to sleep very badly and have the day end 'cause I couldn't arrive at any solution or a focus point to all the things that were bothering me. "Darkness" was just built around that feeling. I wanted the darkness and sleep to take me and just kind of blot out everything and let me rest and sleep and get away for a little while from what was happening.

Jesse Colin Young/The Youngbloods

I love writing, because you leave something behind. You continue to the world of music. For instance, Bach, if he happened to come back, he'd be very happy to know that he lived for all these ages or maybe he died for a while but then came back alive with music of today. Actually Bach had a great influence on the bass players of today. If you listen, a lot of the bass players are playing the eighth notes.

I love doing the funky stuff. It gives you that inspiration, that thing that you just can't forget. But I love writing ballads. For instance, "My Cherie Amour"—I wrote that two years ago, three years ago, and we cut it about a year ago and never dreamed it would be the A side. The A side originally was "I'll Know I Love You." I think it was too early for the record buying people, 'cause it was very funky, definitely funky, gutty, and it didn't really do that much. I think it went up to forty something, but "My Cherie Amour," ummmm, it sold a couple of records. I think basically for a funky thing to sell it has to be really together. Musically it has to be melodic. People like something they can hum, that's got a beat.

Stevie Wonder

I don't write songs very often, so something has to motivate me. Then whenever that does, I'll sit down, and usually, like the span of writing a song, conceiving the musical idea to finishing it, may be a year and a half. But it also might be a couple of hours or a half hour or something. It really depends on the tune. Once I get an idea for the words I can usually go right through it quickly. But it takes a long time for an idea to be congruent with what the music was.

Jorma Kaukonen/Jefferson Airplane

Roger McGuinn

Three years ago I was present at a recording session where the Art Reynolds Singers put together a song which is called "Jesus Is Just All Right," and they had it out on an album on Columbia which was a bomb. I thought it was very good music. And the song stuck with me, and so I decided it would be a little freaky and kind of groovy if we did it. So we did it.

Gene Parsons/The Byrds

"Eight Miles High." We got the idea from listening to John Coltrane in our mobile home. We were driving around in the Midwest, doing one-night things and playing cassette tapes. We had two tapes: John Coltrane and Ravi Shankar. That's all. They didn't make tapes commercially at the time. So we had to record them off records and didn't think ahead of the tour to record a number of things, so we just had two things to listen to, and Ravi Shankar and John Coltrane were heavy influences as a result of that repetition, repetitious hearing of them. We love them, too. The reason we ever recorded them on the cassette in the first place was because we dug 'em. But they did wear well, yeah.

Roger McGuinn/The Byrds

Stevie Wonder

The Approach

In our experience singing, we found that you can't please everybody. So what we're trying to do now is really please ourselves and get a message across to the audience if they'll listen. We're trying to keep up with things that are happening today. Some songs that we sing are for children, for young adults to stay in school, protest songs about things that have happened in the black man's life, and inspirational songs. We still sing our gospel songs. I feel good about what we're doing. I found that by singing a lot of folk songs and the protest songs that we have the opportunity to advance, and we get a wider audience. You know, we don't just sing to just one group of people. Like when we were singin' gospel, we sung more or less to a black audience all of the time. But since we're trying to sing songs with a message, a meanin' other than religious songs, we can spread out. We can sing to college students.

When you're singing about truth, people are going to feel it anyway. They can understand it. The feeling was there, but they didn't know why they were feeling that way. What goes from the heart reaches the heart. This is the way I feel about it. And when you get that goin', then you don't have anything to worry about, because people will follow you. All they have to do is understand what you're doin', and if they feel you, then you have an audience someplace, and they'll appreciate what you're doin'.

Cleotha Staples / The Staple Singers

I'm basically a ballad singer. I like smooth things, things that have feelings and you can get the message across and you can put more energetic feeling to it. When it comes to a fast song, you sing fast words. You're listening to the band. Hey, man, you know . . . "railroading." But when it comes to a slow song, *I get real serious* and I'm really down to earth when it comes to that slow ballad, any slow ballad. If I hear a slow ballad by any artist, it doesn't particularly have to have a "soul" feeling, but if it has meaningful words to it, I dig it. I really love it. I really got to freak out behind that slow song. I love it.

Sam Moore/Sam and Dave

The thing I love is mistakes, because we've come to a point in chromatic music where that's where the new things come from—from overt mistakes. And then knowing how to get out of those mistakes —this is what improvisation is all about. That's what makes a great improviser: somebody who can get into a bind while improvising and know enough to work his way out of it. And that's what makes beautiful things, beautiful solos.

Felix Pappalardi/Mountain

Sam Moore

The Message

We all grow. And this is a time of great creativity. It's a time when people like to feel what they hear in song. I'm just trying to get my wavelength, where I live, where I groove, a little bit stronger, and it's led me here. Instead of its being "Four Women" this year, it's "Revolution," which is not just a comment on colored people, but it involves the whole spectrum of remaking a world for us to live in, and that's what's on everybody's mind.

"Four Women," "Mississippi Goddam" . . . I think I have about seven songs that have only to do with my people. This is needed, but on the other hand, there are other things, there are other revolutions that are going on also. And so, like again, "Mississippi Goddam" was restricted and limited to my people. We need an awful lot of encouragement. We need an awful lot of songs directed to us. It's no more limited than songs that one writes for children or any specific group. My "Revolution," as I see it, is limited in that it's speaking to colored people and white people, and it's speaking about the racial problem. In the song we're talking about remaking the whole Establishment, if we ever get together. There have to be special situations, and that's what Curtis Mayfield has done. I think it's the Impressions who sing "This Is My Country," too. I'm very proud of the fact that I was around a long time doing it before now, singing it before now. I'm just proud that I have seen things come into, attitudes and things being born that I was only talking about years ago.

Nina Simone

If you believe in yourself and you're wrong, but you're not willing to find out whether you're wrong or not, then I say stand, because when you stand you'll find out that you're wrong, and then that'll do you the most good 'cause you'll have to ease over. 'Cause you got to live with yourself. I think every human being feels exactly like that record, even if they're wrong, you know.

"You Can Make It If You Try." It just depends on what you think makin' it is. What means you made it? I really believe you can make it. Anything you want to do. You can just cut off everything, just keeping at what you're supposed to do. But people won't do that. People smoke when they know that they're killing themselves, but they won't stop. That doesn't mean a person is silly, unless most people are silly. You won't stop smoking when you know that's killing you. There are other things that you won't stop because you dig the chick or you dig the guy, and it'll hang you up. And obviously it's hangin' you up, and you still hang yourself up and die with these hang-ups when all you have to do is cut 'em off. So if you try, if you really want to make it, you just cut off everything that ain't doin' you no good. I don't have any hang-ups. I don't do anything that I don't want to do.

Sly Stone/Sly and the Family Stone

"Choice of Colors" was brought about through a question. A question and an idea: "If you had a choice of colors/which one would you choose, my brother?" After I'd come about with that particular lyric and question, it turned out to be more or less my own theory and philosophy as to how maybe the masses or how I as an individual would think from here.

I came back with another question: "If there was no day or night/Which would you prefer to be right?" Here's a song and a lyric that is basically a question to the black masses as to how, honestly, where are you in reference to . . . we know you're black and you're proud and all that, but if you really have a "Choice of Colors," which one would you choose? Which sort of puts you up against a wall. And if you're really where it's at, then you, you know, through your pride in knowing what you are, you would have no fear in saying, "I'm black and I'm proud."

Curtis Mayfield/The Impressions

Curtis Mayfield

I was on vacation in the summer, and there was an assassination. It was a man I really admired. Like Dr. King I admired, but I really didn't know him as much as I knew Bobby Kennedy. We were kind of involved with the Kennedys. We worked with them, and it really just wrecked me. I remember it vividly. The first thing I wanted to do was to attack something or somebody. But it changed me. It really did. And "People Got To Be Free" came as a result. A very frustrating experience. I was looking for someone to follow as far as in the political world, and there was nobody around. It looked void.

Felix Cavaliere/The Rascals

When you get down to the loud, loud rock . . . when you tone it down . . . if you listen to the loud rock groups, when you tone them down, they're sayin' somethin'. The records I really dig. Now I must be truthful with you, there are a lot of them that I would never go see because I could not take it. My ears, you dig? I've been to places where I just had to split because it was just too loud for me, but usually, if you can tone them down, they're really sayin' something—musically—their lyrics mean something for today, saying something that's right down to the nitty-gritty, to life.

Smokey Robinson

Keith Moon

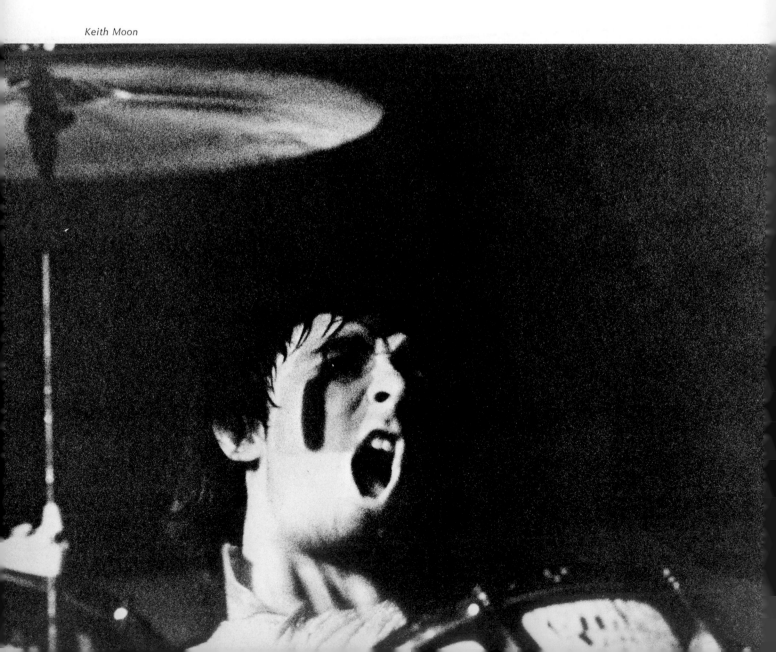

"Boris the Spider." I just had a childhood fear of spiders. In England they always seem to be on the ceiling—always up there. I just described a spider sort of crawling down, and then you squash it, that sort of thing. I don't like name-dropping, but I was sitting next to Bill Wyman one night down at the club, and we started talking about spiders, and I thought of a name for a spider: Boris the spider. Our production manager, the fellow with the bald head, he was driving my Bentley, he said, "That would be a good title for a song 'Boris the Spider.'" I had been contracted to write two numbers on The Who LP by the publisher who had given me an advance, and I'd already written "Whiskey Man," and I had to write another one for the album. And, like, we were recording it at that time. So I thought I might as well settle that and write another one about a spider called Boris. And we stayed up half the night, and I said to him, "How about a chorus going 'creepy, creepy, crawlly, crawlly'?" I mean I just sort of wrote the words and the next morning I got up at ten and did the demo tape of it. That was just the amount of thought that went into it. It was like a drunken booze-up. We just did it as a joke. A joke subject for a number. It just sort of worked out. Actually, my mind was very active at that time. Nowadays it takes me about two weeks to think of something to write about.

John Entwistle/The Who

"Long Tall Sally" was a girl in my hometown, and my Uncle John, and then Mary. They used to keep her and I used to nettle her. I used to call her Slim, you know. Long Tall Sally and my Uncle John used to drink a lot and on Saturdays, you know, you had to get paid on Saturday in the South. And he would go off with his women, you know, and get drunk, and when he'd see my auntie coming, he would duck. And when auntie was coming, he'd duck back in the alley. That's the way I started. It's a long lost story.

Little Richard

John Entwistle

0

Tell you what "Sunny Afternoon" sounds like. I could draw it better than tell you what it sounds like. It looks like a leaf, very sharp holly, and in the background is a big round sun and the leaf is cutting through the sun coming through. That's what it looked like. I said this is the sound of one. I couldn't explain it to the engineer, so I drew it. I said this is how the bass should be, flat, this sticking up in the middle which is the rhythm guitar. I think it saves a lot of trouble if you can do it.

Ray Davies/The Kinks

George invited us to Apple. We went round and then he gave us "Something" as a song. We spent ages before we actually got "Something" together, and it seemed very strange that by the time things worked out, that they both got released about the same time. Paul McCartney was there at that time and he gave us "Bathroom Window." George's version of "Something," though, 'cause like when he gave it to us he just gave it in a rough demo of him singin' and playin' guitar, you know. You couldn't tell that much from it. But I was really amazed when his version came out because his guitar playin' and his singin' both, you know . . . he's come on so much it's incredible.

Joe Cocker

Once you get in the business, you write, produce, and arrange. Then you have that bug to perform. I've been a vocalist all the time. I guess the time ain't been right. So I wanted to take a chance on cutting a tune.

"By the Time I Get to Phoenix" is a great piece of material. I've heard it done by a lot of people. Your soul record buyers weren't very much aware of the tune because Glen Campbell is a pop country and western artist.

I was sittin' in a club one night and went up to sit in with the band. So I did the tune, and I did this little talkin' thing on the front end. The people dug it. People suggested, "Hey, man, why don't you record it?" So I went in the studio and did it, maybe not verbatim the way I do, because each time is different. It paid off because people really dug it and bought it and made me feel good to know that I was a disciple of Jim Webb. . . .

"Soul Man." As you know, within the last few years the black image has come on the scene. It was the summer of '67, and we were sittin' around, so I was thinking the word "soul." I said somebody should really write a song about an individual, like soul sister or soul brother. And I tossed the idea around. I really couldn't get a title. We took a five or ten minute break, so I stayed in the studio on the piano and messed around and came up with the rhythm. And in the rhythm I could hear "soul man." So I ran out and got everybody and pulled 'em back in the studio and cut a rhythm track. Then David (Porter) and I got together and played the track and we wrote the tune. That's how that tune came about. We put ourselves in the position of a "soul man." We had to in order for it to be a good marriage between Sam & Dave and the tune.

Isaac Hayes

"Up from the Skies." Yeah, well, like people layin' up in gray buildings and so forth is dusted away. And people run around shoutin', "Oh, love the world, love the world!" you know. We *love* everybody! Eatin' rodent seeds and so forth. I don't know. You know, even when you go into people's houses, people must respect other people's ideas. Long as it's not hurting anybody. That's all I can say. And they must respect the time sequence. The president once said, "Listen, when it's time for a change, by all means you put that thing in operation." Like why keep livin' in the old, in the past? These buildings ain't goin' to be here for all that long, so why be like that.

How could "If Six Was Nine" be anger? I don't say nothin' bad about nobody. It just says, man, let them go on and screw up theirs, just as long as they don't mess with me. Quite naturally, you try to help people out here and there if they can appreciate it.

Most of the ballads come across in different ways. Sometimes you see things in different ways than other people could see it. So then you write it in a song. It could represent anything. I like to write songs like "Castles Are Made of Sand," personally. When it comes to the ballads, the ballads I really like to get together. That's what I dig.

Jimi Hendrix

Joe Cocker

Some people have accused us of being bitter for writing "Rock and Roll Star." It's no more bitter than "Positively Fourth Street." In fact, it isn't nearly as bitter as that. We were thumbing through a teen magazine and looking at all the unfamiliar faces and couldn't help but think, "Wow! What happened? All of a sudden here's everybody and his brother and his sister-in-law and his mother and his pet bullfrog singing rock and roll." So we wrote "So You Want To Be a Rock and Roll Star" to the audience who is going to be potential rock and roll stars, who were going to be, who would like to be . . . and some did realize their goals.

"Mr. Spaceman" is a funny little song based on my interest in space, probably a result of my interest in physics and chemistry. I was fascinated in school with those subjects. Those were the only subjects besides music that I got good grades in. As a side note, I happened to meet a cat, an astronomer, who heard "C T A 102," which was an album cut that we had about a quasar. His name is Gene Epstein—Dr. Epstein, you know. He's a young cat, and he likes to be called Gene, and he likes to hang out. Well, I've been out to the Aerospace where he works, out to his radio telescope where he has . . . you don't see anything. It's all computer readout on neon pilot tubes with numbers, and he's got a slide rule there, and a pencil and a piece of paper, and he punches buttons on the computer and types things into it and moves the scope around following quasars, studying their path and trying to find out what they are. Now, I still think they don't know exactly what they are. Then they discovered pulsars after that. I met a number of other interesting people in the field of astronomy through him . . . got into that field. So it paid off to write some songs about space.

Roger McGuinn/The Byrds

The *Berkeley Barb* ran a page—sort of an ad—of a collage with a lot of words on it and pictures . . . you know, those Italian Westerns, the movies. Remember the villain in *The Good, the Bad and the Ugly?* The bad guy. They had a pictures of him in a long trench coat with his gun drawn and shooting at a big hat, and it said, "We are outlaws," and it had a lot of phrases that are in the song "We Can Be Together" in there. And it's sort of a paraphrase of that and a couple other things that I drew from other places. But a lot of it's word for word from that: "We

are all outlaws in the eyes of America; in order to survive we steal, cheat, lie, forge, hide, and deal." It was turned around a little to make it rhyme in the right places.

David had that melody for "Wooden Ships" for about a year. Couldn't write words to it. Steve and I and he went down to his boat one day after Steve broke up with Judy Collins and needed somewhere to go and work it out. We just finished a tour back east, so I went down, and we just sailed around and wrote the song. . . . That's what we thought about when we did it—it would be a nice thing. 'Cause we do it totally differently, it's nice to have a song that way.

Paul Kantner/Jefferson Airplane

Jorma Kaukonen

Eddie Brigati

"Nights in White Satin" was written by Justin while he was sitting on the loo in his flat in London. We rehearsed it in an old broken-down church—and then basically—purely for a song to do on stage because we badly needed new materials for our staging. And the arrangement just came. We just played it as the way we felt it and then recorded it that way. And that's the way it came out.

Moody Blues

I see nothing but gypsy people on the road. And gypsy is America today, the new and the live America. You say, "Why do you call yourself that? Why don't you get a strong name?" Forget about . . . we have to relate. You have to give 'em a name that they know, you know. So like "Little Wing" is like one of these beautiful girls that come around sometimes. They might be spaced. They might be, you know—kind of strung out on a certain this or that.

You know everybody has a right to their own releases or their own beliefs, if they want to believe that a star is purple or whatever. And like these girls, which is one girl to me, it's like "The Wind Cries Mary" is representing more than one person. And like she's the one that really comes around. Put it in another picture. You ride in town; the war happens. You ride in town for the drinks and parties and so forth. You play your gig; it's the same thing as the olden days. And these beautiful girls come around and really entertain you. You do actually fall in love with them because that's the only love you can have. It's not always based on the physical thing of "Oh, there's one right over there. Let's get her (plah-plah-plah-plop)!" You know, it's not one of those scenes. They actually tell you something. They release different things inside themselves, and then you feel to yourself, "Damn, there's really a responsibility to some of these girls, you know, because like they're

Johnny Winter

the ones that are gonna get screwed." There's a lot of discrimination on women today, anyway. But just don't let 'em have too much, because some of 'em will go crazy (laughs)! "Little Wing" was a very sweet girl that came around that gave me her whole life and more if I wanted it. And me with my crazy ass couldn't get it together, so I'm off here and there and off over there.

Jimi Hendrix

"Johnny B. Goode" was one of the first ones I started doing, when Chuck Berry was the Jimi Hendrix of those days, when I was just learning to play guitar. Everybody in the world played "Johnny B. Goode." It was really weird the first record that I made because I won some kind of a little local contest in conjunction with the movie *Go Johnny Go* with "Johnny B. Goode." Chuck Berry was in the movie and like it was a talent contest; the winner got a big recording contract with Dart Records in Houston. And so I won the contest and it was really strange, the whole part of my early coming up was associated with "Johnny B. Goode."

Johnny Winter

The rock songs started talking about some of these gut-level, balls feelings, which is what existence is really about.

Lorin Hollander

It just happens when it happens. Usually, though, I write a song because I need one. I tell myself I need a song. Then I write it. I kind of commission myself to write songs, you know. But it makes it easy because there isn't somebody else telling me I gotta write a song. So I can do whatever . . . you know, I can do any kind of song I want. Sometimes I write with the idea of its being a single or a stronger tune or something. Most of the time I'm just experimenting, trying to write something I haven't written before.

I'll write melodies or I'll write music, and at the same time thinking about things I'd like to write songs about, and eventually they come together. Sometimes from three totally different things that were halfway developed on their own, and then I stuck 'em together. A lot of times, the music's all done, and then I got to put something in it, what it is about. "Proud Mary" was that way.

Actually, the song "Green River" had been there

Eddie Brigati

for years and years, and when I was really young we used to go up to a place near Sacramento. Pewter Creek was the creek, just a little tributary of the Sacramento River. Anyway, there was a little place there called Cotty's Camp, and I only remembered that there was one cabin. Tom tells me that there were more. But when you're four, your world's about this big. And all the things in the song are there. I didn't realize 'til I was older that everybody's got a place like that in their head, someplace. Even if they were never there, they saw it in a movie, and they thought it was neat. So when I wanted to write a song about it, I just wrote down, not melody or anything, not even rhyming words. I just wrote a little story of all the stuff that was there: gravel roads, and the dirt roads, barefoot girls, and the whole works. Just kind of stuck it in there and then started taking out the key things that gave me the most impact, that I didn't have to explain. Everything in that song is right up front. There's no mystical meaning at all. It's just right there. It's kind of a romantic thing. Because, I think when I was seven or eight, they had the water project come in and wipe the whole thing out. The title "Green River" really came from the drink, Green River. When you turn the bottle upside down, the label's right side up, like at the soda fountain. On the West Coast I see 'em all over the place. It's just like a water cooler thing or a cherry Coke . . . the same thing. It had a little picture of a sunset and it said "Green River." And then it had the river going to infinity and little trees and stuff on both sides. When I was about seven or eight, I saw it at the local pharmacy for the first time. And I thought, "Wow! That'd be a neat name for a song." And I always told myself someday I'll write a song called "Green River."

"Lodi" is a two-way deal really. It was a very peculiar problem to musicians. You don't find that kind of thing much in anything else, except maybe migrant farm workers. But also there was a greater thing involved with everyone who's stuck in his respective system. More people I think know about the pitfalls of show biz than any other type of industry. But everything you do for a living has its own built-in limitations. I was talking about both those things at the same time, the fact that you can have all these promises and hopes and all that crap and still maybe never get anyplace.

There's some things I don't like to take apart, 'cause they mean a lot of things to a lot of people and I want to keep it that way. "Effigy" is on about four different planes, and once I tear 'em apart, the parts don't quite equal the whole. They really don't.

John Fogerty/Creedence Clearwater Revival

John Fogerty

THE PERFORMANCE

I think to entertain is an art. The ability to entertain is like the complete statement. And it's an art form because everybody can't do it. You can be an artist and not entertain, but it's pretty hard to entertain without bein' an artist. Whatever that is! I hope I said it right. You know, like I go to see a magician, right. Now magic is basically all chicanery and entertainment. But the guy who really does it great, man, is an artist! And you know it's all tricks, and you know you're bein' put on, but it's the way you're bein' put on that's a gas, you know! It's like eating is entertainment. So you eat to survive, but like you go and you see all this beautiful food and it looks too good to eat! And you eat it and it tastes better than it looks! The cat that prepared this is an artist. He's not just a cook. He's an artist.

I would rather be an entertainer than an artist. Because an artist makes his statement and he makes it for himself and to himself, and if you like it, good for you, and if you don't like it, sorry 'bout that. But not really, because, like he's wrapped up in his own thing. Maybe he's so intense or so involved in what he's doing at the time that nobody can dig it but him. Then fifty years later they discover that what he was trying to say was hip. Whereas on the other hand I see an entertainer trying to communicate. You know. His whole thing is to communicate. And there's nothing greater than communication. To me, communication is where it's at. It doesn't leave you hung up. It doesn't bother you. Some people get a kick out of being hung up, I guess. Which is why they try to find geniuses and people they don't understand so they can figure 'em out.

Jerry Butler

I'm in this thing of being able to communicate with a lot of different people. I don't want to be an exclusively hippie-appeal person. But I'm not going to get slick in order to communicate with all these jive people that have to see you go from a funky cat to somebody like Bobby Goldsboro, who's changed his image with hair spray and shit like that. I won't do that. But I do want to reach everybody. When I write my book there's going to be a lot of pictures and a lot of drawings and simple words, and I'm not going to use any big words like I learned in college because you only communicate with a certain amount of people, and you cut out a lot of others, and I'm not interested in that small number any more than I am with any other groups of people. That's why I like simple music, because in the first place I like it better and in the second place just more people can get into it than they can the other thing.

Elvin Bishop

Gladys Knight

We started a school at Motown called Artist Development, in which our artists learn choreography and harmonetics and things of this type to carry them over in the entertainment world because there was a time when our field of entertainment had become so lax none of the nice spots wanted to buy it. It was just junk, you dig? People said, "Oh, that junk!" They didn't want to see it or hear it or anything, you know. But today at Motown we feel that you should entertain people when you go out. Because your great people do: Frank Sinatra, Sammy Davis. You go see these people. They're entertaining. They're not just there singing songs, you know, which is what our brand of entertainment had fallen off into, you know. I am very happy to say that now, more so than when we first started, the younger groups who are coming up now realize this.

Smokey Robinson

I'm not known that much as a musician . . . more of an entertainer. I might think of myself as a musician, only it's not that noticeable because I entertain. I enjoy entertaining, but I wouldn't like to entertain and not be into what I was doing. There is a compromise in music. You can't just do whatever you feel like; you can to a great degree, but you've got to compromise things to some degree to present it.

Alvin Lee/Ten Years After

I don't give a damn about visual things, you know. It just happens it's part of the music. I don't need to explain it or talk about it. I don't care. I don't place a high value on it. I've ceased long ago to even think about it. After I was aware that I did it, and found out why I did it, then I stopped thinking about it. It's not part of theater; it's an extension of music. It is the music. You know the music and that are the the same thing, the same emotion.

Ian Anderson/Jethro Tull

Jimmy Page

Jerry Butler

Paul Horn and Donovan

We doin' better than any other gospel group on the road. Nobody like nothin' dead; the thing got a move to it. Church people like to clap their hands —not anymore, that's a thing of the past now. You can't do the same thing you did ten years ago. That's out. You've got to be emotional. You have to entertain now.

Pop Staples/The Staple Singers

There's a thing that happens, confidence happens, after a certain degree of success. In other words, after having played for an audience of half a million or like five million that I just got through playing for tonight ("The Tonight Show"), you have this confidence that is almost unshakable, and all nervousness leaves you. It becomes a perfectly natural act to play for a lot of people. Whereas I used to make my best music alone in my home because I had to adjust to living before the public. To really do it before the public, without being up-tight, it's a matter of confidence. At this point in my career, I have a lot of confidence in myself. Because not that much more could happen, except more of it. Differently, certainly. I couldn't play for many more people than I have played for.

A really nice, free, beautiful scene can happen anytime, anyplace. Always. You never can tell what you're walking into. I mean we get these jobs, and they're always for some reason, you know. I mean, we don't know what they are. To us, they're places on an itinerary. But when we show up, we often find out that they're for a reason. Somebody's holding a festival, or somebody's holding a fair, or they're celebrating this or that, and that's why we were hired to play there. Sometimes it turns out to be really great, sometimes, really stiff.

Barry Melton/Country Joe & the Fish

When I go to a concert I'm a big success. "What a great professional performer he is." That's not it. I'm onstage and I can open the key for twenty thousand people to express what they have inside them. They're sittin' in the dark thinkin'. They're listening, but they're opening themselves completely, and I'm just drawin' them out, man. Because it makes us feel good, beautiful, amazing.

Donovan

Everything is changeable. Like nothin's going to stay the same forever. As I learn somethin' I'm goin' to put that across in my music. But it's easier to listen to music with words than it is to just listen to somebody talkin'. And I figure I could get across on the stands better through music than through talkin'. It's not my thing to talk. My thing is to make music.

Dr. John, the Night Tripper

I don't like making albums for transistor radios and things like that. Our major problem is getting a record to relate to what we do "live."

Alvin Lee/Ten Years After

The Voices of East Harlem

John Kay

Sometimes I'm like very up and I'll go through a whole bunch of things if I feel good. And at other times I'll be very lumbering, kind of. It really depends on how the sound is—like how good or how bad it is. There were times, like in concerts in Europe, when it just got so frantic and I was throwing microphone stands around and twirling things. I broke several microphone stands. Not in terms of taking them and crashing them, but I was just ripping on them, puttin' my foot on them and bending them like a pretzel. At other times I may remain almost motionless or may not even say anything at all during the entire set. It really depends to a great degree on the audience reaction.

You see, the only time I see myself is on the tube. The tube always makes this mistake of shooting from the waist up, so all you see is this head going back and forth. Like a pendulum. I know that I have certain tendencies, like to have my head down a lot, but I really don't know how it looks from afar, the entire group, collectively. I don't really dance, mainly because I'm just too big for all that. You've got to be a certain size to look graceful to go through those kind of changes, and I never felt . . . rhythmically I'm not terribly well coordinated. I can sing rhythmically, but you really have to have a certain feel to go through these gyrations and execute them like a dance contest, you know. And I don't like it too slick. And none of the guys in the band go through a slick trip. That's one thing that we're all similar in, depending on what the circumstances are of any one given performance. That's how they will move, or if they will move.

John Kay/Steppenwolf

One of the things . . . every time we make a record, we go through a . . . we go on a trip of "Wow! Think of what we can do with a record! Here we are in a studio where we have total control over all the sound. Sixteen-track machine! Why, we can drive people mad with what we can produce in here!" And so it gets like that, and we get like just crazy behind it, because we don't have a producer, and we all mix it. It's like sometimes there're ten hands on the board, groping and struggling and bringing up certain sounds, and the result is that there's no center. Our records are some experiment that we've never gotten off behind. We never have gotten on. We almost got on once.

Right. But there's a "live" album comin' out pretty soon. So that's us "live." At least it was a year ago. Nobody's heard us play like that unless they've come to see our shows.

Jerry Garcia and Phil Lesh/The Grateful Dead

There's no audience that you can't get out of their seats. If you got it on, I don't care who it is, man, you can tear ass. You can get 'em up and dancin' and smilin' and just lettin' loose. Man, they're free. Lots of places the cops stop it.

Marty Balin/Jefferson Airplane

Pete Townshend

If the people move, when you can see the people moving, you play better, or you play more solidly or more rhythmically, and they move more solidly and it just keeps increasing. It's a quality factor somehow. You get bodies and gravity working together and your rhythm moves in from a physical plane—I mean coming from physical laws that are pretty subtle. The only way you can experience rocking back and forth is rocking back and forth, and then it's like a lot of forces are being moved into play. And that's like a thing that hits you. That could be a definition of what a groove is.

That's what the people were into then. They're not into that anymore, except around the edges, even in San Francisco, but you can see 'em move. Their minds move.

People stopped moving when the rock bands learned to put on a good show.

That's part of it. And the whole fame trip came into play—the East Coast influence, the draw thing. All that got everybody into thinking of the trip and going to a show to see blah-blah instead of going to a dance and wiggin' out. And it made it different for us, too, and then we had to go to a gig.

Right. Because then there'd be stars. We played out at the Pavilion here last time we were here, and there were a hell of a lot of people dancing, just about everybody, in fact, and I think that stuff still happens when it's the right situation. You can't very well dance on the front of a seat. It doesn't promote that when you're sitting on a chair. There's this big funnel down to the end of the stage. You're focused that way. It's just a whole different thing.

Jerry Garcia and Phil Lesh/The Grateful Dead

The Sam & Dave Revue

Robert Plant

Sly Stone

Before most black acts go onstage they go through a tremendous verbal battle with each other, where they really put each other through a lot of changes, funny changes, but still like "who's that girl I saw you with last night" stuff, and they get to a together point before they play. I don't know if this is consciously. There's a tremendous difference. When you go on a stage, if you can go on a stage as a group, you can conquer any situation, any situation, even like when an instrument's gone. When you go on as individuals, you can't do it.

That's really what we're for. I mean, that's our role that the great force has given us. We're entertainers. We have a point of view, which may or may not be important, depending on who's listening, but the music is the reason that we're here. The entertaining. We're supposed to make people happy. That's the most important thing. When you hear music you're supposed to enjoy it.

Felix Cavaliere/The Rascals

Somebody actually said in the English papers . . . they put a picture of me and said, "Cut it out and you got little loose arms and you can fasten strings to it: Joe Cocker puppet." Which is about as far as you can take it. I don't care. It's something I started doing because I don't play anything. I didn't want to start doing the old Caruso bit. So I started picking up on what the instruments were playing. Which helps to keep me in tune with what's going on. Some nights, if everything's going well, it feels really natural and good. And it's only if I'm feeling a bit stiff for some reason I can't go into it, but it's getting better all the time. I might pick up on the guitar or organ or whatever catches me ear at the time, or if anything's . . . like the drums . . . if it feels as if they're lagging me, I sort of try and give them a tug along.

Joe Cocker

Vanilla Fudge

What we all fail to understand is that the majority of rock and roll stars are diaper people, relative to how to handle an audience. How long have some of the great money-earners of today been in the business? You have a Hendrix who knows how to handle crowds, but he is still basically a shy person. And if something goes wrong, it's like a . . . like a great comedian when you get a guy in the audience heckling you. You know how to handle a heckler.

But generally speaking, there has been an improvement in the stage presence because a tree grows . . . human beings grow just naturally. But even the beginning groups are learning that there's more to it these days than gimmicks and show biz or frayed costumes or things other than music. I think more and more of the groups are aware that a stage presence is needed, especially in the major cities. I like to think that although a guy can be a fifty-thousand-dollar-a-night level and a mummy, he should want to be more, even though he's at the top. Therefore, because he wants to grow as a person, as an artist, he should want to improve.

Bill Graham/Fillmores East and West

The Fillmore East has a light show because the audience has eyes and the musicians don't always know it.

Kip Cohen/Fillmore East

In all of our backgrounds, if you had to look for one common thing, it's theater. We all have a certain theatrical discipline. Whatever the problems may be, at a certain time the show has to go on, and the audience has to see something which relates to the audience—not our own trips or our own problems as to what we feel is groovy at a particular moment, which is what we feel is a mistake most light shows make. They go on their own trip and they completely forget the audience.

Tom Shoesmith/Joshua Light Show

Jim Morrison

Sha-na-na

We like to do something new every week. Not necessarily a new effect, but a new approach to something, something which, when used in the show, will show us a new technique.

Joshua White/Joshua Light Show

We shy away from doing very experimental things because the audience only sees it once. It finally winds up like the high art approach where you try a lot of things and reject them and finally wind up with something very good. We're delayed by the exigencies of having to get the show on every week. Gradually, sometimes with frustrating slowness, things do work their way in. It's been building ever since then. We have a lot of frustrations right now about things we think could be better, but which we can't afford to do right, so we haven't done yet. This is from a lack of time, equipment, and personnel.

Tom Shoesmith/Joshua Light Show

Right now we're a business. We're almost like a service. We provide entertainment, visual entertainment for the people. In addition, we'd like to have this thing evolve into a fine art product. Meantime, we've got to be financially responsible and all that sort of thing. We have to balance it out. Sometimes it's a drag, being in the business end. And other times it's nice to get paid every week. So it works out both ways.

Bill Schwarzbach/Joshua Light Show

We don't like light shows. It usually turns out that the light show is a distraction, especially when you want to put on a show and you look around in back of you and there's all these weird colors and oils and things . . . listen to the music and trip on the colors . . . forget the dudes on the stage . . . they're anonymous . . . no involvement . . . it doesn't touch your body . . . no interaction with your neighbor . . . the psychedoolie culture.

MC 5

I like light shows. They have to be run just right. The music tells a story and lends a certain kind of physical surrounding, and more often than not you don't get what you really want. It's hard to notice onstage what lights are coming down and how it looks . . . the total picture.

Jerry Goodman and Jerry Smith/The Flock

Ian Anderson

Wayne Kramer

152

A film background is definitely one element. That's why I think the show was able to do as well as it did. Tom and Bill and I each brought to the show very distinct skills. And each new person that gets involved brings other skills. My skills are in business, graphics and photography, in film making and television. Bill's skills were in lighting, technical theater. Tom's skills—we're not quite sure—he does good things, and it's the same as Bill's, and whenever we work behind classical music, Tom dances it out for us!

The ability to create for the need—and the need at this theater is to create instantly. Anybody could do what we do, but I don't think anybody could do it the way we do it, how we do it, when we do it, and for the money we do it.

Joshua White/Joshua Light Show

The Kinks

Mick Jagger

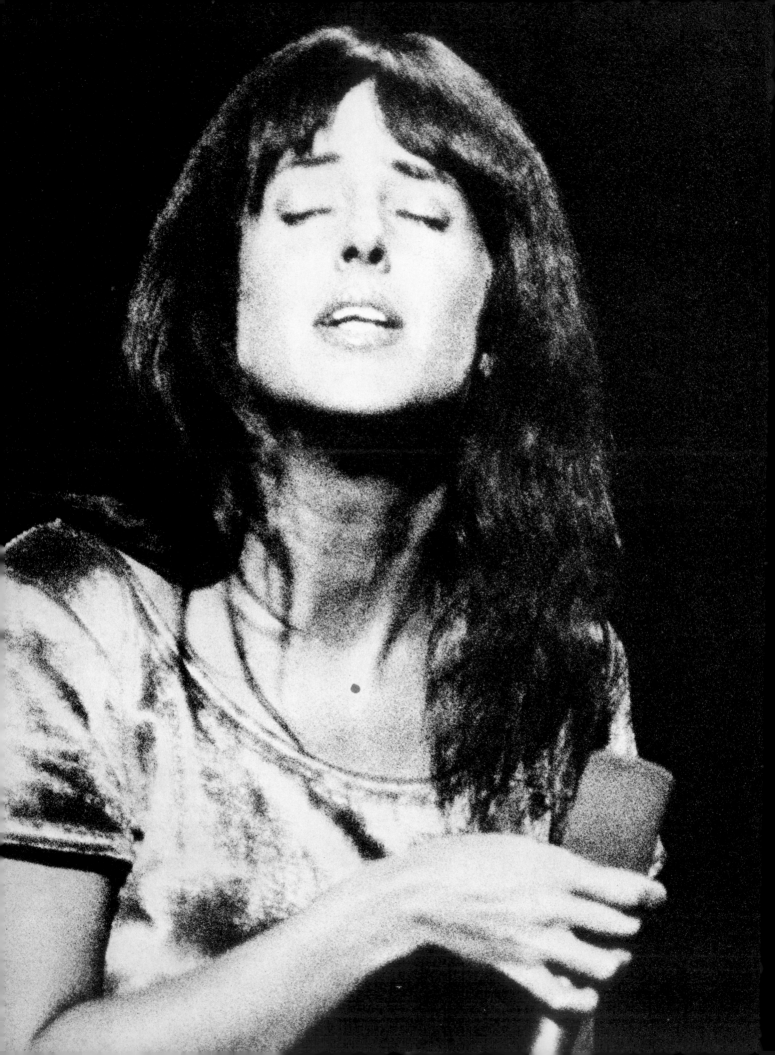

I hate for little kids to come flashin' on me sayin', "Oh, wow! You played great tonight!" knowin' all the time you played bad. That's because they're flashin' on me. That's too much burden on me. I'm just like them. Forget about names as long as the whole stuff is constantly moving toward gettin' things together.

I don't disrespect them. I appreciate it, but it hurts me almost inside sometimes. That's just my own little hang-up, though.

Jimi Hendrix

We don't want the music to suffer to have a show. If it's gonna be one or the other, we take the music any time.

John Fogerty/Creedence Clearwater Revival

The only way a person can stay in this business is to enjoy what they're doing and I think my responsibility is to give my best recordwise and performancewise. If I enjoy it, I don't stop to think about it.

You can't eat before a performance and little things bug you. You get up-tight easily.

Yes, every performance is like your first one. 'Cause you've got a new bunch of people, and you know that there's somebody in the audience that never saw your performance, just heard your records. Sometimes you get a few that never heard your records either.

Moody Blues

The Liverpool Scene

Grace Slick

On a record we might emphasize a certain point or a certain passage or something. Might have the drums or the guitar swing around to the other side with the echo goin' the opposite way. Some people say this is gimmicks. We don't need that. We don't do it in person. In person we play it maybe a different way. So for the record's benefit we just try to take you somewhere far as the record can go. It does call for a switch in this and that and makin' that sound like it's coming up and down and so forth, just to emphasize the song.

In records you can do almost anything you want.

But then in person, like with the three-piece or four-piece, you know, with a small group, you're not actually tryin' to get that same sound, because that's been had on a record. You can leave the concert and go home and play the record if you want to hear it just like that. We give you another side of it. We play outside . . . that's another side of it 'cause the air does something to the sounds . . . and then you can just go on and jam with it. I don't know, it's better playin' in person for, I guess, anybody. 'Cause you can just raise hell if you want to.
Jimi Hendrix

MC 5

The Grateful Dead

It's fun to play at little funky clubs because that's like a workhouse. It's nice to sweat. I remember we used to play sometimes . . . even the amplifiers and guitars actually were sweating. Everything is sweating. It seemed like the more it got sweaty, the funkier it got and the groovier. Everybody melted together, I guess! And the sound was kickin' 'em all in the chest. I dig that! Water and electricity!

That's what bein' a musician's about . . . is just playing. Playing anywhere. That's why we can play Madison Square Garden and come down and play at the Experience, then go back over and play the Whiskey and then play Hollywood Bowl. See, once they get all those ideas about what buildings is which, they're sayin', "Oh, they'll play down there, it must not be very good because they're not known to play there!" That's silly. It's fun anyway to me. It's groovy that we get paid. All the kids have to remember is regardless of where you're going, just check it out. You've gone there to hear the music. It's terrible to have to rely on the Madison Square Garden all the time. 'Cause those places are not for real good rock music. Then you have to go to the small clubs and get your ears blasted away. I think they should make special buildings, like they make special buildings for restaurants and hotels. They should make special buildings for loud, or whatever you want to call it, electronic rock music.

Jimi Hendrix

I think the human race is just about to grow up. I think the human race, if you'll pardon the analogy, just came for the first time. I think that they sent their male symbol to the moon and did their female symbol on the pasture in the same year. That's all on very magical level symbols, but we did get off this little blob of mud for the first time, and go somewhere else. Actually go there and come back, for the first time, the same year that we all got a whole bunch of people together and proved we could actually live with each other.

David Crosby/Crosby, Stills, Nash and Young

Crosby, Stills, Nash and Young

Jimi Hendrix

I'm so turned on to America at the moment I can't tell you. I really . . . I really got me fingers crossed, and I'm touching wood. Because it's, it's precarious, but it looks like the weight is going on the right side of the balance at the moment. I'm an eternal optimist.

Graeme Edge/Moody Blues

In American riots you see these masochist kids. Some of 'em will say, "Well, we don't have nothin' else to live for anyway. This is our scene now." They go in there with no shelter, no anything. They get beat. I mean you can see, you see how desperate the whole case must be if a kid's goin' to go out there and get his head busted open. Without no protection. Just gettin' things together. But then you look over in Japan. Now these students got it together and you must put this in the book, 'cause I'm tired of seein' Americans get their heads split open for no reason at all. The kids in Japan, they buy helmets, they got their little squadrons. The pink helmets for the left side, and they go in wedges like this. They got all their stuff together. They've got their shields. They're wearin' steel supports— protection. You have to have all these things if you're goin' to go up there; you might as well make it together. Just go on and do it together. I'd like to see these American kids with helmets on and big giant Roman shields and then do their thing! Really together. America. That music is goin' to tell 'em anything they want to know, really.

Jimi Hendrix

I think the significance of rock and roll for myself, and a lot of the people who are very, very good in the production end or the business end or the music end, who came from the theater world, is its very spontaneity. No one knows the next step. I don't know where it's going, but it's taking everybody somewhere. You sort of trip with it.

Howard Stein

Neil Young

Jethro Tull

An ideal thing would be to go onstage with absolutely nothing in your head, and everybody get together and pick up his instrument and play and improvise the whole thing—lyrics and vocals and everything, whatever's gonna happen—and have it come out just as boss as you could want. And perhaps that's a place where we can all get. But it's in the experimental stage.

It's kind of like an alchemical experiment that you have to repeat. Again and again and again, the same experiment, exactly the same or as close to the same as you can get it really. But naturally our music isn't like that. We don't repeat the music—the details of the music—over and over again. There's a framework for that, too. But it's like the same effort. The effort is to get higher.

Jerry Garcia and Phil Lesh/The Grateful Dead

Today, music is getting to be such a broad thing. That's all there is today—music, music, music. People listen. I imagine if political people decided to put their speeches to music instead of just saying them, they'd get heard a lot better. Say, for instance, say the President makes a speech and they put some *bad* music behind it. Everybody would listen to that. I know I would. I'd sit down and listen to that one time just to hear what's going on.

I'm saying how hip the kids are today. They're smart. They know every word. As a matter of fact, the teachers complain and say, "You can learn every word in that record, but you can't learn in my class." Maybe they ought to put their lessons on records—with music. Then they'll dig it.

Gladys Knight and the Pips

In the future I would like to conduct an orchestra, and I'd like this orchestra to be made up of younger people, some of the freaky kids from Juilliard who happen to dig the violin rather than the guitar, the cello rather than the drum, and put together a group of these kids and play Mozart and Bach and conduct on the keyboard, or conduct some of these . . . these magnificent baroque statements. Let the kids see some more of their counterparts up there playing these sissy instruments . . . effete instruments.

Lorin Hollander

John Mayall

FESTIVALS

When festivals are run properly, they are beautiful because there's a lot of people. And, you know, the more the merrier. I really like the idea of a lot of people together enjoying themselves together.

It's a psychological attitude. Everybody's the same, sitting together. There's a physical contact if you're sitting close together rather than in a movie seat. And you're out there in the hot sun and you know what you came for. Everybody's having a good time. Beautiful.

Jerry Goodman and Jerry Smith/The Flock

The kids get together. It's a good thing. It's a cultural event. They should have balloons and clowns.

MC 5

Woodstock was groovy and all that, but anybody can get a field and put a lot of kids in there and put band after band on. I don't particularly like the idea of groups after groups. It all starts merging together. They didn't give a damn about the sound equipment. The people way out there that couldn't hear nothing. So when you do festivals you're either going to have to have more days or offer them more things besides music. You know, you should have little booths where they can buy this and that, where the Indians can come in and sell their jewelry. A little circus here and there.

It's very hard sometimes. If you look out there and see . . . if there's about two hundred people in front of you, you know good and well that those people way out there are not going to hear anything. Unless we're down at the Bowl. I had a lot of fun at that Denver, Colorado, place. We played out there at Red Rocks. That was groovy. That was nice. 'Cause people are on top of you there, or at least they can hear something. That's where it should be, natural-theater-type things.

Jimi Hendrix

Jorma Kaukonen

Just the conditions of festivals, especially Woodstock, aren't conducive to movin' 'cause first you have to concentrate all your energy to see the band 'cause they're only this big and you can barely hear them anyway, so you're not gonna get deep into it or involved or moved. And second will be the dope which certainly relaxes everyone, but I don't think that dope is goin' to be more powerful than any rock and roll band any way you look at it on any level. And third would be that the show isn't on-stage. Just look around at all the people. I think that the energy—another possibility that the people at Woodstock didn't go wild—there ain't a whole lot of bands that are into movin' people. I think that the bands that did the best there were The Who and Sly and the Family Stone. Those were the bands that were into movin' people. They were the best received.

MC 5

Music festivals are currently a very popular thing, and I can't really see it from the angle that people who come to see and hear music can see it. I could never be in that position and understanding what they like about it. But I can see the kind of . . . it's like a fairground sort of event. It's exactly that. It's a festival. But from a musician's point of view, it's a sort of hit-and-miss thing, because when you get that many names all put together, and bands—there's so much involved in the organization of such —the organization can sometimes present problems that wouldn't normally happen if you were just the only band in a club or a concert somewhere, where you have far more time to set up and get conditions right for your own particular performance and play for as long as you feel like playing. Whereas festivals are usually things where you're just another name on the bill, and you have to rush on and rush off and you really don't get time to settle into an extended musical performance. And you're off before you do anything, and they're shouting for more and there's no chance of giving them any more because the next person's got to come on and he's going to be subject to the same conditions. But they can be . . . they have a good atmosphere, which is really exciting, and people really enjoy them.

John Mayall

Mavis Staples

It's like the money thing of it. Everybody wants to get on the bandwagon. They don't give a damn about those kids out there. If it rains, well, it rains. If it does this, well, it does this. The way I could see a festival is have a little circus thing over there, have a little tent area, where you have tents you could rent out to folks or whatever. You have music goin' on at certain times, and then you show films at certain times. You have dances and arts and maybe even a play. Yeah, exhibits and so forth.

This summer's goin' to do that about twice as big. Three times. I bet they're going to have more than a million at least at one or two of those festivals this summer. Like I say, as long as it's done up for the idea of enjoyin' and pickin' up on good vibes. Monterey was great. It was a predominantly music festival done up the way it's supposed to be done up.

That's our start in America. I didn't know too much about festivals and all that, except I used to go down there at jazz festivals. Beyond that, it was great. I was scared to go up there and play in front of all those people outside. Everything was perfect. In other words, I was scared at that almost. I said, "Wow! Everything's together! What am I gonna do?"

Jimi Hendrix

The worst thing about festivals is that they're poorly organized as a general rule. The first one I ever did was Monterey, which was well organized. That was dynamite. But there are only two or three that even come close to that comparison. How many festivals have there been? Thirty? Forty? It's hard to count. But we played twelve or so last year, and at most of them finding the stage is a problem. Finding someone who knows how to get backstage is a basic problem. You get there to this big racetrack or wherever they've rented some land. And knowing that you're not getting out to the people on the periphery, on the edges of the festival, is sort of a drag. You know they can't possibly hear you. They can hear a little muted sound coming off the stage and see some little figures up there. It's a weird feeling.

Roger McGuinn/The Byrds

The festivals we play now are usually very clever ways to make ends meet for a number of people. It seems like it should be based on a theory that you do anything you want as long as you don't hurt anybody. Then it's all right. If everything was free—everything, all the food, all the talent, all, everything. Everybody should chip in—in an organized way. Everybody should chip in. And give everything—free all day and all night. And the only thing to be given, maybe, is credits for what group of people gave it. You can't always give credit by name, and the people that do those kind of things don't really care if they're named anyway.

Sly Stone/Sly and the Family Stone

TELEVISION

The problem with the television industry is that they are on the level of ownership and directorship. They are inextricably involved in the power structure. They have that FCC gun at their heads. And therefore, they control and censor themselves, even more thoroughly than they need to. And they, at this point, feel that they have to be watching their step even more than usual because everybody's watching 'em. See, we've cracked every other medium, dig it. We've cracked all the others. With TV we are still limited to sneaking little nuggets of truth into the garbage stream. It's very difficult. It has to be very underhanded. We only get to do it in double entendre, except for a rare occasion where someone in a moment of usually instantly trampled liberalism will let us speak out for a minute or two.

We should all try very hard. But don't expect them to change, because it is not in their interest to. And interest is a mighty motivating force. Particularly in a bureaucracy. Bureaucracy's self-interest, its main aim, is self-perpetuation and self-interest above its stated aim.

David Crosby/Crosby, Stills, Nash and Young

We haven't done any TV so far because it's the medium we know the least about. It's the hardest to do well. It seems like there's a lot of older people in TV that really don't know what they're doing. Like they get a rock and roll band that plays very loud and they don't understand that and they say, "Well, you don't have to play that loud." They don't understand. They don't know the proper way to mike groups, and it's just a big hassle. We haven't done any major TV. We're waiting until we can get big enough to do a good major show and maybe produce eight minutes ourselves or something like that where we can make sure we've got the right people in there and do it where it's going to come out right. We're really uncertain about it, so we want to make sure it comes off right the first time.

We want to make sure we can go in early, rehearse it, and if there's any problems with lighting or sound, maybe even get our own lighting and sound people in there. We haven't gone into it to the point of where we really know exactly what we want because we haven't gotten that close to it, to

where we've actually gotten down to the . . . well, you know, we'll go on if you do this, and it just hasn't worked out perfectly yet so I don't know really exactly what we're going to want. But it's got to be. It seems like it would be hard to do a TV thing because it would take more than two or three minutes. It would be hard to capture anything like the kind of stuff we're doing in two or three minutes. So I'd rather wait until we can get at least eight minutes.

Johnny Winter

Television blocks people's minds from thinkin'. People can't sit down in a house where they got a television and sit with the television off, sit down and talk. You know why? 'Cause it's too hard to do. It takes thinkin' to sit down and talk about something. And we're like babies. We're spoiled. We got to go to the television. It's like our bottle. You can't get away from it. It's sad. I remember when I was a little kid, everybody after dinner would sit down and talk about things. We were talkin' and gettin' ideas across, and everybody's mind was workin'. But you sit in front of the television, mama puts the baby in front of the television, and mama sits in front of the television, and daddy sits in front of the television, everybody—all strung out on television. Somebody got a six-hour-a-day television habit, somebody got a twelve-hour-a-day. Next thing they do, they're goin' to have to have a hospital for people to go get rehabilitated from television! It's sad. Television is much stronger than any narcotic drugs. Cigarettes and booze and all that, but ain't got nothin' on television. It's sick.

Dr. John, the Night Tripper

At the very outset of our career we were kind of imprisoned with our attitudes, you know, "There are certain shows that we're not going to do, like Dick Clark. We're going to wait for the biggies!" And we found that that is just so much bullshit. The people that we want to reach watch Dick Clark. And we found that we've done Dick Clark now about six times. Dick Clark has been without a doubt the most courteous, most cooperative, and least censorship-minded outfit that we've ever done anything for on the tube.

John Kay/Steppenwolf

David Crosby

171

PRODUCERS AND PLACES

Bill Graham and the Fillmores East and West

I think he's an excellent concert producer. I think perhaps he and I are the only concert producers in New York, as opposed to promoters. A lot of things I do, with alterations, have been influenced by the things that Bill Graham does. The high regard for professionalism and discipline—words that are nonexistent in rock and roll—that he tries to institute into the Fillmore and his operations, I agree with. His respect for the artist as an artist, even though it's rock and roll music that he's playing, I agree with. I think he's a fine producer. I think he has great musical taste. Good understanding of chemistry of music, of one band counterpointing another on the same show. Things that most people don't think about, he thinks about. So, professionally, I think he's like an excellent concert producer. Personally, I've always had problems with him because we're competing.

Howard Stein

I think that the difference between like myself and most of the people that I see in my "field" is that I'm a . . . maybe I'm just a disguised thirty-year-old red-blooded American boy. I'm an athlete. That's what I dig about Bill Graham. I can go out to the Fillmore West and I can shoot baskets with Bill Graham for four hours . . . and he's good. He can handle himself. He knows how to move. He knows what a jump shot is. I mean, he knows how to do it.

Felix Pappalardi/Mountain

The business of rock in general—and it is a business—is much more competitive. There are many more people involved now because people have found out that it's profitable and therefore it's much harder—the business. We're not talking about competition. I mean good and bad, positive and negative. Even if somebody opens across the street and if the person opens across the street and he's very good, he will, in order to succeed, have to do a better job than we do, and therefore the community is richer. But if somebody opens across the street and fails, even in his failure he hurts us because he may have offered a five-thousand-dollar act ten thousand dollars. Because he gave them ten thousand dollars he may have gone bankrupt, but we'll never get that act back down to five, because they said, "The last time we got ten thousand dollars." So competition has made life harder.

It would be great for me to do a commercial for the Fillmore and say, "Yes, that's right. They love everything, because we do everything beautiful—peace and beads and love." I think what you run into is that on the weekend that a particular group or particular program is presented, the ones who come are the ones who love those particular groups. And they stay away on weekends when that which is being presented they don't love. It's like running a restaurant. On Monday nights everything you serve is good and on Monday nights you have roast beef, Tuesday nights you have chicken, Thursday nights you have Salisbury steak, and every night you're full. But the roast beef people come on Monday night and on Tuesday night come the chicken people. And every night, everybody sits and says, "Jeez, I just love chicken; I just love roast beef." But the chicken people stay home on roast beef night. Which may blow everybody's mind. It's so easy to say that everybody loves all the shows we do. No, I assure you that the Crosby, Stills, Nash and Young devotee is not a Vanilla Fudge fan.

We cannot just put together great shows because then you go bankrupt. And it would be nice—and I've said this enough times also—that one of the joys of running this place or the two places . . . I wish I were government subsidized or state subsidized and then do like Bergman does or Polanski did before he came over here and make the "films" I want. The government pays hit-or-miss. It's just good stuff. And yet by being competitive and not

Felix Pappalardi

172

selling out, you can attempt not to change your tastes but to change their tastes, and then it all falls in line.

That's one of the joys of having your own place, not being strapped with unions and having groups who dig playing. The Airplane this weekend . . . they blew my mind. Five A.M.—whatever it was. That's one of the joys of the business that some of the groups who can do their forty-five–minute concert, stretch them to two, two and half hours, three hours . . . the Grateful Dead, Crosby Stills. That's one of the reasons we've been able to hold onto some of them. But everybody thinks it's only from the business point. It's very sad and difficult for us to continue because a half a dozen groups that we'll never present here again because of the dollar . . . the business has gotten so big. At one time four or five years ago it was from the Matrix to a thousand-seat hall, to a . . . to the Fillmore. Now the Fillmore to the Felt Forum to the Garden to the ocean to God knows.

My feeling is this, and I know this sounds like back-patting, ego, self-commercialization. There's a place here and there's a place in California and there may be another good hall somewhere—you know—Chicago, Detroit, some other dance hall or concert hall. And if I were the manager of a big group I'd say, "Jesus, and boys, you've got to rent equipment. In Detroit we got to find a place and make sure that the guy's honest and in another place we play municipal auditoriums and commercial venues and whatnot. But I would like to think that when I get to New York there's a twenty-five-hundred-seat house, and the sound is there, and the lights are there, and the people care, and we can do production numbers and visual effects and stretch. It's a gas." It's a very simple, simple feeling. An act comes in here and says, "Bill, we want the drum on this level, we want the lights to come in here and we want, when we sing a song about Chicago, can you have a film on slums or whatever?" And in between shows we'll show a Looney Tunes cartoon or play bingo or whatever it is. To be able to experiment.

Bill Graham

They have an incredible staff over there. 'Cause we went in on Friday night, last week, and it was a scary thing to play the Fillmore 'cause we hadn't been together that long. The first night we played too loud. We really did. They called up the next day and they worked with us, and we cut down the two tops and three bottoms Saturday night and we were great Saturday night. Of course, they helped. They could have just said, "Well, forget these dudes." But instead they were very conscientious.

Felix Pappalardi/Mountain

The Pavilion

The Pavilion was a success. The notion of taking a monstrous place and getting as many people as you can, and in uncomfortable seats or bleachers, and having them pay much, much, much more money than they should have to pay to hear rock and roll music, and then leave after two hours when they should be beginning to get involved in the music that they're listening to, and go home and have a hot dog off the stands and an orange drink, I think is a drag. A total drag. I think that slowly those kinds of places will fall if there's competition in town. I think we were our own competition, incidentally. I think the Pavilion being ours as well as the Singer Bowl, that showed the public as well as us that we were doing something so exciting, and why would anything so boring (Singer Bowl) right next door to it survive?

I don't know how I got the Pavilion, but I know I strongly believe in the freedom of it, the space of it. The basic beliefs about production, the kind of thing that we wanted to do, the kind of atmosphere that we wanted to create. One of the differences between promotion and concert production being that a producer doesn't have a concept behind it all. It's more than a matter of getting them in and getting them out and getting your money. It's a matter of what kind of set do you want to leave them with, what kind of a point about music, or about audiences, or about audience participation in music do you want to make.

I think, I'm beginning to believe . . . well, a lot of things are beginning to happen to me . . . my way of doing business and my business thoughts. I think that music is part of something that even as a

David Ruffin

whole is more important than music. I think that in a way it can bring people together as it has at Woodstock, in some indescribable way, the way it did on weekends on a smaller scale at the Pavilion. I think it can leave them with the notion that they're part of something that's bigger than music alone. It sort of reinforces your belief in yourself and that you're part of a community of selves who have positive things to say and do and freedom to experience things like that . . . and the kind of space and openness. I mean the Pavilion is open. So is the generation that comes to the Pavilion. There's space. There's undefined opportunity to move or to sit . . . react. It's not an establishment. Your reactions aren't established for you. You don't sit here or clap there or get up and leave and get your program and walk out. So I think in a sense it's making a statement about the people. Right now music is the one thing that it all has in common. I think that there are other things that are going to develop about beliefs and philosophies and working together to build something.

Howard Stein

Carnegie Hall

Carnegie Hall constantly objects that you're bringing rock and roll back since the Beatles. They maintain, and I don't know why or how, that they've always accepted good music of any kind on any level. They keep on screaming every time they read a review that says rock and roll comes back to Carnegie Hall. I don't know. I think to an extent that there's probably a financial motive on their part. It's not as exciting as the Pavilion. It's not the perfect way to hear rock and roll. It's a more qualitative place than most of the halls in New York City. It's not scary, you know. You don't walk in and feel depressed instantly. There's something pretty about red carpets and Austrian, nineteenth-century balconies, loges, dress circle . . . you know. There's something pretty about that. It's not like walking in some of the strange places—armories and things—that people find to do concerts. There was also a kind of excitement about bringing rock into Carnegie Hall. It became significant, a corny word, but it became significant that rock and roll was in Carnegie Hall. It was off limits until we did our show there. Again, it was a way of expressing—this audience that we were talking about, young people, people who were interested in music—concerning our music is good enough for anywhere, and Rubinstein can be heard there. There's no reason why Led Zeppelin shouldn't be heard there. I'm not making a comparison. It's just that it's a kind of musical declaration of musical independence. On a small level. Probably more private to me than to the city at large. Led Zeppelin sold out in advance, of course, but they won't let me have standing room. You can have standing room for a symphony orchestra, but they still don't trust . . . they won't let me sell standing room.

On our first concert our stage manager set up all the equipment for the Flying Burrito Brothers. And the union head came up to him and said, "You'll have to take those amplifiers off the stage." And my stage manager said, "Well, why do you have to take them off?" And he said, "Because they're pink and that's not aesthetic!" So if you have any artistic questions that you want answered, I can tell you who he was, and you can go down and ask him—like if a painting looks good in your home!

Howard Stein

THE AUDIENCE

Everybody in this generation can't be a musician, and that's what they all want to be.

But they don't understand. It doesn't spring up overnight. They think, "Oh, God, a rock star. Look, they get to look freaky and take dope and they're rich!" It seems like the dream life, man, and not everybody is equipped to be a musician. If they want a new society and if they want it to work, and they want it the way it should be, everybody's gonna have to do what they do best. There's gonna have to still be plumbers, man, and doctors, you know.

Audience

It's good to see people yelling. Twenty years ago nobody said anything. I like it when they say something. It doesn't matter what they say. It saves people from going out and stabbing somebody, if they can get it off. Somewhere, just yelling out. Maybe it does, I don't know. Maybe those are the guys that go out and stab people, that yell. The entire auditorium is a bunch of killers (laughs). It's also the people on the stage.

Grace Slick/Jefferson Airplane

The Flock

It's sort of like a baby grasping for the tit. A lot of kids today are completely moved by their sensations. They want to be pleased. They're very hedonist. They want to be satisfied. It's because they—so many of them—have been on a certain sustained level of satisfaction their whole life. When they leave their families, they expect it. They expect it from the society because they got it from parents.

Audience

A bodyguard at a religious service—how about that!

Cleotha Staples/The Staple Singers

I don't know what draws it. I just reach up and feel it. It draws it . . . they show that they dig it, and I hope I never lose it. That's all I can say. But I have wondered why. Because you have two forces, you have a force goin' up, and you have a force that sits back and listens . . . it makes you feel good. The other part makes you feel just as wonderful, just as good.

It's really beautiful, though. And I be tryin' to keep singin', but you can't shake hands with everybody. Sometimes the audience don't know how hard they are pullin'. Like I got cut here. They weren't tryin' to pull the ring off, just pullin' the hand. Like all the scars on my hand are from fans. They love you. And nothin' is wrong with it. 'Cause I have done the same thing. I have walked in this Apollo Theater, and I walked up and shook Sammy Davis, Jr.'s hand. There's nothing wrong with that. I collect autographs. I am the biggest fan of a lot of singers. The fans that do run up to the stage . . . I think it's beautiful and I love it.

David Ruffin

We're proud we're an English rock group. The audience likes us, and we'd like the audience to like us every day. We like standing ovations and all that, but if you don't do a good show and the audience give you a standing ovation, you don't think in your mind, "Oh, perhaps it sounds a whole lot better to them, you know, offstage." You only think of how it sounds to you. And if you haven't done a good show, then you think like, not exactly like takin' the mickey out of you, but bein' sympathetic. I mean the worst thing for a rock musician who's standin' there, sort of really playing hard music, is sympathy from the audience.

John Entwistle/The Who

Somebody just said something that was with me, man. People come up to you like you were somebody up on a cross. They just want to touch you. They don't want to hurt you. Nobody tries to take anything. They just want to . . . it's a heck of a feeling. It's beautiful. I can't explain it.

It has been that way ever since I was with the Temptations. There wasn't one particular thing that started it off. It's hard to explain. The feeling that they're giving is just a wonderful feeling. It's hard to explain, but it's there. I can feel it. When one of those kids grab my hand, like this—not "come here," but . . . if four or five grab it, you know it's gonna pull. It's not that they're trying to jerk me off the stage. I would love to believe that whatever I am delivering to them, whatever I am giving, I think the same feeling is coming back into my show.

David Ruffin

If you get a clever audience, they can make you collapse.

Alvin Lee/Ten Years After

My responsibility to an audience is to do an honest job of trying to communicate with them, to give them some kind of value for the money they paid. So it's rather a disappointment to me when I feel I haven't played my best through things like bad P.A. systems or an incorrect balance or various things like this which restrict you in your creative performance, and then they applaud like mad, and you don't feel it was quite worth it, 'cause you'd have loved to have them hear it much better, but at the same time that was the best that you could

David Ruffin

possibly have done under those circumstances. So if you've got those attitudes always, then that's fine, because that means that you never think you're any better than the next man as regards playing. You're just somebody who's trying to play music, and you never reach a point when you think, "I'm so-and-so, and I'm infallible, and I can afford now to do, you know, to forget about the audience." You've always got to feel when you go onstage that nobody's ever heard you before and that you've got to try and win an audience purely on musical efforts.

John Mayall

I'd like to know . . . I mean, they don't have to scream, but at least the applause at the end of the show. And I do like excitement. I'm a bull—Taurus.

Stevie Wonder

We look at our audience; they're paying the money; we have to do the show. Whatever it take to attack an audience mood to make them come up, we never want to see them in a mood, but we want to get them up because this is what they came out for—to have a good time and to see two people who are tryin' to and makin' an endeavor to make them happy.

Sam Moore/Sam & Dave

Rapport with the audience, you dig? I mean, I love it! I love it! I swear, I mean I just really love it!! Oh, I can't explain. There are no words I could really give you to explain how I really feel when this is happening, especially if I think the people dig it. If they're having a good time, I don't care if they applaud, whatever . . . you dig? If they're having a good time, I love it.

Smokey Robinson

Sons of Champlin

The Voices of East Harlem

You really want to turn those people on. It's just like a feeling of really deep concern. You get very intense. That's the way I look at it. That's natural for me. Once you hit the first note, or once the first thing goes down, then it's all right.

Let's get to those people's butts! That's what I want. We used to say a thing like, "If you don't have no blues with you, we'll make some to take home." That's goin' to be our theme. Not sad blues, you know; blues today.

Jimi Hendrix

I find differences with audiences. It's like the towns vary from the west to the east. Obviously the different conditions people live in affects them. And if you get in towns sort of like Philadelphia or going up to Minneapolis, or places like that . . . Seattle, you know, there's definitely a different mood up there in those sort of places. They're not as tuned in, but you can't expect them to be because they're so far away from the centers like New York and Los Angeles. That's generally why there's more kicking off in those towns. It's just because that's where the pulse is. Sometimes we do a good show and if we don't get off, if we never get to that point, it upsets me as much as it upsets them. I love sit-down audiences, you know, 'cause it's a big challenge that people just sit there and want to listen and be taken over enough to get into it. So it's more of a challenge than having people . . . well it isn't really . . . 'cause I mean if people are dancin' about, you know, you really haven't gotten their attention.

Joe Cocker

The public overall, I think, from the young kids on up, the buying market, has certainly become much more educated. Their demands are for better music, whether it be psychedelic or whatever. Whereas songs during the fifties were truly what you might call rock and roll, you know—basically two or three chordal changes with two or three lyrics that are repeated. Nowadays you don't have that. So I think everybody is definitely showing a true appreciation for original creative work.

Curtis Mayfield/The Impressions

It's hard to determine what's goin' to be getting you across. Record sales, and when people turn out, you know you're gettin' across. You know when they stop doin' that, you might as well forget it. As far as somebody comin' up and shakin' your hand, they can't let you know nothin' about that, except that they just want to meet you, just see you. A lot of 'em are curious what you're like. I think it's curiosity. They're just curious what you're like or how you'll react . . . something like that.

Wilson Pickett

Barry Melton

Joe Cocker

Jim Morrison

At Woodstock, they were mostly . . . weren't interested necessarily in what was going on onstage, it seemed, but it seemed like they were mostly interested in each other. And themselves. That was the thing. That's what's so great about it. The music was there to provide a reason for going there. Okay, you got to have a reason to go there. Come on, here's an excuse to dig each other. Boss! Let's have more of that!

I'll buy that. I like to think that there's a trend toward people wanting to get into their bodies, and they go and listen to a band, to dance, rhythmic, and they can do things with their bodies. There's evidence of that in some areas. Kids are going to get into dancing, giving up their energy and doing things with it. That's what we like. If you have an audience out there that's giving, too, that's dancing, you can work together. They give and you give. And it builds up and at the end of the night it's like a climax.

Phil Lesh and Jerry Garcia/The Grateful Dead

The main thing is you should communicate with the people who have come to hear you and that they should identify with what you're doing if it's at all possible, and the audience should be as much a part of the music as the actual musicians that are creating it before them.

John Mayall

The reason they listen so close is because half of them are . . . a lot of them are . . . musicians. So many. And that's good because they want to hear good music.

Clarence White/The Byrds

Once in a while you get an audience that claps right on the back beat, you know. I think it was at the Fillmore East one time that it was really hip. They helped us. Sometimes when they clap, it is rough to play against it, 'cause it's off.

Gene Parsons/The Byrds

We have watched our audience grow, and they've watched us grow. They've watched us a little more perhaps. Some of the letters that I used to get and some of the letters that I get now are quite different. And like every once in a while, two letters or three letters will come in that somebody really got the message. It's really funny because they will send a letter like and say, "I'm twenty-one, and I've never written a fan letter in my life, and I don't know why I'm doing it," and when they get through with that trip, then they finally tell you, "I just want to tell you that I finally understood what you are talking about, and like it's beautiful and I'm going to start reading and studying" and things like that. And it really makes it all worthwhile. Because sometimes you wonder whether people are really listening.

I mean they've been brought up to understand what to do when the music gets good, whereas a white person cannot release his inhibitions, although, you know, it's changing . . . it's changing. Sly Stone is doing a fantastic job of changing it, too. He says, "Look, I know all about this and how good you look and everything, but forget it for five minutes," so people are learning. There's a tremendous difference in an audience. It's more felt rather than seen. You can feel it, you know. It's people singing in key . . . things like that.

Felix Cavaliere/The Rascals

Mick Jagger

A few years ago the traditional all-American-boy image was almost all over the place. You know, everybody's skin shined. In those days you weren't allowed to smell of perspiration, but you were allowed to be slightly damp, which, of course, is totally unacceptable nowadays. You just have to drown in your own juices.

And from there to the end is where we are really at. And that's what we want them to listen to. As for jumping up and doing encores, I don't think we're the greatest one in the world. I don't think anybody could find it possible to our music. Because it's just not that kind of music. And if the greatest fan in the world really wanted to, we couldn't do it because . . . you've had tempo changes too many times.

It's a weird situation to be in, because you don't want to go on, and yet in the same breath you don't want the kids to think that you're putting them down or that's what we was paid to do and you ain't getting no more. Remember that.

We're too big time to go back and perform for them. But that's not the case at all. It's just that it takes our enjoyment away. And the only reason that we're here to play is because we're happy and we're going to stay that way.

Moody Blues

So I say that we're God's bouquet. We're just like the rose, the lilies, the sunflowers, the medallion.

Little Richard

Little Richard

You find that it's much groovier, whether you be watching a performer or whether you be performing yourself, to truly put your whole mind and body into it and clap your hands rather than sit there idle and just listen. . . .

I like to sing for kids. They sit there and they have this big smile on their face, and maybe if you look down at them or smile at them they just crack up. It's nice. I really enjoy it. You see, now, as of this year, we seem . . . we . . . like are drawing a more younger crowd, too, now, where a while back, it's like mostly adult audiences that we didn't do all this dancing and going on, and it just wasn't there.

Well, I would imagine this has got to be about the most understanding and appreciative audience when it comes to songs, whether it be through love, faith, messages, or protest. These people are open-minded enough to understand other people's situations, as well as lots of them have their own personal feelings as to his surroundings, the country, current events, local situations, as well as national problems, and these type of people . . . they don't have any barriers against something that one may want to say in reference to his own hang-up, you know, because they can understand it. So they really enjoyed what we had to say.

The Impressions

The Apollo audience will accept anything that's presented well. This is probably, can be, the worst or the greatest audience in the world. 'Cause if they dig it, they let you know it. And if they don't, they let you know that, too. And they let you know it right away. They don't mess around. They don't all sit there and then say, "Well, let's see what everybody else does." If they don't dig it, there's "Booooo, get outta here!" And like if they like it, like that cat up in the balcony, he's clapping all by himself. He don't even care—"I like that." Which is beautiful.

Jerry Butler

You should be aware of the audience and you should play to the audience, but you shouldn't go into any phony show-biz-isms. There are so many clichés. All them isms. It's just phony. Sweating in place. Bowing in place. Ending the song in place. It's corny.

Ever since the beginning of 1968, it's been great. We were able to do to the audience what we wanted to do to 'em. It's like we're doin' it to ourselves, too. It's like Carlo in San Francisco where we started. Then our first Fillmore things, the Avalon. People got behind it. They liked it. Before that it was kind of hard. Nobody really cared that we were there or not. I do admit I can't blame 'em. There wasn't enough to keep 'em going. Like we do one good song out of twenty maybe. We didn't realize it then, of course. We thought those people are all screwed up. They don't know. We couldn't compete with things that were really happenin'. I find audiences are pretty honest. It doesn't happen for you before you're ready for it. And they ain't goin' to give it to you until you do it to them. But when you do do it, they'll let you know about it. If I had only known that five years ago, it would be different, because you blame it on all the wrong things. The lights are bad . . . none of that stuff matters if you're playin' real music. They're gonna dig it.

John Fogerty/Creedence Clearwater Revival

There is a change in the general attitude of the listening audience to rock, pop music. It's hard to call it rock because it entails so many different forms, because of the great number of people who have joined in on the bandwagon. The bandwagon is getting heavy, and the spokes are starting to bend, and the wheels are starting to crumble. However, pop music will continue regardless of the bandwagon. It has changed. People have become more blasé. They're harder to impress. They've heard more people 'cause there're more people out there doing it. An analogy that I immediately think of is the folk scene during the early sixties when it sort of diminished. It's gradually happening to rock, though it's bad PR to say so. But it's the truth. I don't know where it's going. I didn't know where it was going when we started, either. It just happened the right way.

Roger McGuinn/The Byrds

INDEX